Beloved

...by this they will know

A transformational guide to living and Loving as Christ.
Change your Mind... Change your Ministry

CHARLES GOSS

eg books
... an eternal perspective

For permission requests, write to the publisher at the following email address
bythistheywillknow@gmail.com

BELOVED...by This They Will Know
A transformational guide to living and Loving as Christ.
Change your Mind...Change your Ministry

ISBN: 978-1-54390-344-7

eBook ISBN: 978-1-54390-345-4

Printed in the United States of America

© 2017 by Eddie Charles Goss IV

e.g.Books
Visit us on the web for booking and other information:
www.charlesgoss.org

Editors:
K. Franks, J (Betty)Rodriguez, Virtue & Amy Sue

Acknowledgements

~ To my **Wife**, **Jennifer Goss** (Virtue), you are truly a virtuous woman whose price is far above rubies. Your support and communication has been an invaluable asset to my life. Only the Father could have fashioned such a partner and allowed me to benefit.

~ To the **Lynch Family**, who loved through the trial and error of understanding these truths on levels that only the Father could ordain. You are **forever** Loved and Appreciated!

~ To **Amy Sue**, a true covenant Sister **'the Genuine Article'**. Our incessant emails have finally come full circle Sis! May the Father grant your heavenly account an equity stake in the fruits of this work ☺

~ To **Henry**, thank you for helping to make it all happen. May the Father increase the measure of understanding and grace He gives you in this season. I greatly appreciate our friendship!

~ To my **ORU family**, (B.Peterson and R.Cartledge), without your consistent inquiry about the book, I do not think it would have been completed. May you experience the fullness of the Father in your relationships! ... Thank You both dearly.

~ To my **Sister Sophia**, whom carries a measure of **Agape** rarely seen this side of Heaven. Our interaction always provide revelation on how the Father desires His children to Love one another... You and D' are truly an inspiration. ~ Thank you for being you!

~ To my Dad, **Eddie Charles Goss III**, whom in raising me, demonstrated the power of the Love of a Father. I pray my children see your same zeal and unselfish compassion in me. I Love & Appreciate You.

Render therefore to all their due:
*... **Honor to Whom Honor is Due***
———
Romans 13:7

Contents

Introduction

This book was birthed from two very common relationship experiences. One type of relationship exemplifies Agape intimacy in a true covenant connection, and the another type of relationship often filled with fleshly manipulations, baggage, and selfishness often fueled by an over-sexualized culture. There is a programmed responsive behavior being sub-consciously taught through social media, TV, advertisement, cinema and music, and no one is immune to its doctrine. As a result, we frequently witness pastors, parents, family members, friends, siblings, teachers and many affluent fall victim to a low level school of thought that is increasingly becoming widely accepted as normal. If we continue down this path, not only will this allow the disease of lower level thinking to spread throughout our community culture, but soon the healthy mind will become obsolete and those operating under this 'new normal' will control the scales of judgment and destroy the fabric that brings balance to our innate longing to connect.

As a young man raised in Southern California, I lived in a loving home with two outgoing parents. By the time I was a teen, my birth mother passed away and the reality of my world was challenged as I began to seek deeper connections with female friends, leaders and co-workers. These connections would identify a common voice heard in story after story from my female counterparts. Time after time they would seek a connection that was deeper than sexual attraction. They desired a father figure, or a brother to protect, cultivate or shield them in times of distress only to be met with a male mind that was not understanding of his role. It seemed that most of them carried the same experience of manipulation and/or perceived sexual mistrust by the men in their lives. It mattered not if they were non-believers or avid church goers, the sickness seemed to bind story after story to the same cultural fabric of lust and manipulation of familiarity. On the other hand, when speaking to male counterparts about women, the conversations almost always had an unhealthy undertone of sexualization.

As I listened to both sides, I began to see the cause and effect of each reality where both sides were victims of an overtly sexual society and thereby left with a severe imbalance in the places where connection was needed most. Realizing that I wanted to see things differently, I began consciously reprogramming my mind instead of adapting to what had become the norm. Over the years, this awareness of thought uncovered the fact that in my sphere of influence, I was alone in my beliefs. I decided I could and would make a change to consciously stand out even if everyone around me acted contrary. At the time, I did not realize the scope of what that actually meant, but starting with my youth group and relationships around me, I began to change the way I interacted with both men and women. Around men, I strived to become more of a representation of what I thought a man should be. I became more outspoken encouraging them to view women differently. Contrariwise, around women I no longer looked at them through the eyes of a person solely of the opposite sex, but I began to view them as sisters. I began to see them as a part of me, as if they had my same family name and we both experienced childhood from the same household. This allowed me to interact with my female counterparts through a new filter of protection and cultivation. The more I did this, the more I became aware that I actually played a major role in their emotional development.

In every relationship connection, we can choose to either dig a deeper emotional hole for one another, or we can be conscious to assist each other in achieving our divine assignments. Once we adopt a conscious awareness of how and why we connect, we can begin to abort the programs that are culturally and systemically destructive. This consciousness will help us become aware that through every over-sexualized interaction with one another, we place a damper on our future desires to be open and vulnerable. This makes it very difficult to grow in positive intimacy, accountability and meaningful interactions. As humans we were created to connect with one another and bear each other's burdens in difficult times, not make the journey of life more difficult. Family is one of the most important microcosms of support and emotional stability. The possibilities of who we call family is greatly increased through our faith and reaches into other continents, ethnicities, creeds and genders.

Beloved, it is critical that we are able to Love boldly and purposefully without fear in this modern age. We should engage relationships in the Light of truth and learn to avoid walking in the shadow of the fear of darkness. Women *need* Fathers and Brothers; and Men *need* Mothers and Sisters. Let us confidently progress past the fear of lust and secular manipulations, and establish the bonds of intimacy and true connection that bring much needed healing.

Preface

Regardless of childhood background, status or faith we all have experienced the broken family structure. This has left many with the feeling of being orphaned. But despite the brokenness, the heartaches and the deep emotional wounds, true Love is more than enough to fill those gaps. We were created with an eternal command to bear the burdens of another and to esteem others higher than ourselves. I pray this book encourages you to Love wholly and unconditionally those around you, regardless of sex, race or creed. Let us understand how to walk in the Light, and begin to demonstrate the operational and functional role of those who first Loved us.

Beloved, let us Love one another... eg

1

Accommodating Fig Leaves

Admittedly, what you are about to read within these pages may be controversial or even seem quite dangerous to most readers. Equally understood is that most of the content will be demonized or dismissed because of various cultural reasons. However, it all settles at the reality that we all are still finding the best way to accommodate our 'fig leaves' inherited by a fallen nature in the Garden. Though we say we are free in Christ, we are the redeemed and we are the Light of the world, we are about to take a practical journey into the application of these proclamations. A lot of what we adopt as common behavior will be challenged. Scriptures that you have read will be applied to situations we face each day to challenge your current mindset and stir up the gift of Christ within you. Hopefully you will begin to identify situations in your life where the Father is calling out to you and saying, "Who told you, you were naked?" This is a call to think differently about what is inside us, put away the fig leaves and walk in the fullness of our internal connection.

I remember traveling to the Middle East for the first time as a youth. My friend and I both in our early twenties, traveled from the United States to the United Arab Emirates with a layover in the UK. While in London, we received word that the leader of this trip who was supposed to meet us in Dubai was severely delayed and unreachable. Apparently there was some sort of unrest and communications were down all over the country she was traveling from. My friend and I didn't think much of it until we arrived in Dubai and exited customs. All around us were many different nationalities and races of people, and most had on their native garments. Seeing everything from keffiyehs to dashikis on what seemed like several hundred people was very overwhelming. However, knowing that there was something on the inside of us greater than what we faced brought peace. As we sat down, we decided that we would pray 1 John 2:20 which says, **20 But you have an anointing from the Holy One, and you know all things.** So we prayed that we would receive this unction from the Holy One to know who was there to pick us up. After we prayed, my friend stayed with the bags while I left to go get this individual. As I stood on the airport side looking over the walkway from customs I saw many nationalities. Dubai is a Middle Eastern country but has an abundance of every nationality that reside there. There were persons of Asian, African, European and Arabian decent and we didn't know what type of church was hosting us, the name of the person, name of the organization or what the person looked like who was there to pick us up. Looking out over the walk way I again asked, "Holy Spirit, who is here to pick us up?"

Immediately, as I looked up, an unction came. "It is him". At that moment my eyes met another gentleman's eyes who just happened to be looking at me. The secular mind then said, "That is just the first person you see. Don't be dumb." So, I continued to scan the crowd. I saw many people that looked like ministers in the crowd, but none of them gave an unction. I did however hear the voice of our enemy. He was taunting me and mocking my desire to 'hear' from God. "Who do you think you are?" He mocked, "Elijah?! Paul?!" I could almost hear audible laughter and began to allow these darts to take root. A secular mindset began to rule my countenance as more impatience was birthed. We were going on 15mins and according to the enemy, the Father had not come through. I even began to walk outside, hoping to get closer to the individual and maybe feel something. But all I felt was ridiculous, insane, vulnerable and HOT! So I cried, "Lord, you said, through the unction of your spirit I would know all things. Why have you not spoken?!" He quietly responded with, "I already told you."

I was immediately confused. My mind so convincingly reasoned how the first person I heard something about was simply the very first person who I saw noticed me in the crowd. Now 20 minutes later, I was sweating and complaining to God about something He already answered. I walked up to the man, introduced myself and met the person sent to pick us up. This was the first person I approached. There was no guesswork.

This was the manifestation of laying down my fig leaves (fallen nature), practically applying scripture and walking in the mind of Christ.

I share that story to encourage you. This Love walk is likewise a mentality shift. Scriptural truths that we have quoted for many years, will be tested. As in my 1 John 2:20 story, many of us repeatedly recite scriptures out of familiarity. However, they cannot and will not wholly benefit us or others, until we practically apply them in our daily living.

As with any supernatural work of the Spirit there will be opposition, and we will need to defend our position against the enemy and oftentimes, to our own brethren, but the goal is still to reach the Lost by walking out the written word of God. This mindset is not something we can attain or earn, but rather something we exchange. We are walking in the exchange of our 'fig leaves', for the manifestation of His internal presence or 'Light' within us. It costs nothing, just faith. Jesus already paid the cost for us to be free from the bondage of a secular mind and walking in the flesh, we simply need to learn how to walk in the exchange and properly defend the exchange, and our impact of effective ministry to those we come in contact with every day will exponentially increase.

The cross gender analogies we discuss are honestly just a back drop on which to juxtapose the culture of the secular mind/works of the flesh, against the mind of Christ, or the fruits of the Spirit at work in us.

The actions to Love another regardless of gender, race, creed or belief may be considered dangerous acts when judged from a mindset that is still trying to accommodate 'fig leaves'. This fig leaf mindset is a recreated spirit that uses the cares of the world to hide itself from the true nature of the Creator. This fallen nature has been force fed sexually sensual narratives through casual media, advertisement and entertainment and finds it hard to now operate as Light. Because of this, the implementation of the principles we discuss may seem 'on the edge' to a secular mind influenced by our cultural sexualization. However, the goal of this reading is to find ways to appropriate the mind of Christ and showcase how someone operating truly **free** from the fear of darkness looks at various real-life situations.

When the first Adam fell into temptation in the garden, he ignored our Father's voice and ate of the tree of knowledge. From that point forward, man was disconnected from internal relationship and like the serpent said, became like God, judging what is good or evil all by himself and within his own reasoning. With this realization, Adam, after being naked and unashamed for so long, now chose to use fig leaves to hide himself from God. Seems silly in hindsight thinking we can use fig leaves to hide from an omnipresent God, but when we think we know anything apart from direct communication from Him, we operate in error.

The subject of gender relations will give us opportunity to follow a journey into what the 'fig leaf' mentality suggests. It forces us to examine the influence of our past experience and exposure to secular media, and compares these actions to what the mind of Christ suggests through His written word. We all know what fallen man and putting on fig leaves looks like, but what does operating without eating of the tree of knowledge or what we personally believe is, good or evil, look like? We will find that it is much different than what we experience currently. What we will aim for are the practical actions of a modern day recreated man as we dissect what this mentality looks like.

My sincere belief is that you will receive a deeper revelation of the mind of Christ and how it conducts itself totally autonomous from the secular judgments of what is considered good or evil. We will journey the way of a mentality that chooses to operate as Light first, before ever giving darkness a voice.

Again, this reading is by no means written to provide justification for the flesh to get closer to the opposite sex. In fact, it is the exact opposite. My personal testimony of living in this understanding of being the actual Light of the world allowed me to be married as a virgin, and as of the first publication of this book, my wife and I are going on over 17 years of happy monogamous marriage. Even more so, though my wife and I do not have a formal organization or relationship specific ministry, together we have touched the lives of countless marriages and singles regardless of race or gender, just by living ordinary lives, every single day.

You too were created to touch everyone you come in contact with. At the gym. At the store. At the mall. You were made to be the salt of the earth, the Light of the world, and the Love of the Lord, and so everyone you meet is needful of your fruit. It behooves you to gain understanding on how, in *every* situation, are you going to operate as the Light of the world. The aim is truly to say, "Yes, I have fallen short in darkness many times, but my past does not determine my future. Let us discuss what actually **hitting the mark and not missing the mark** looks like, and do **that**." Yes, we may face a few Goliaths. There are many people qualified to slay giants in life, but often withdraw themselves from the battle because of previous experience. These experience of defeat can often leave a lasting sting that creates fear of future failure. Fear is the author of the fallen fig leaf mindset. Fear is what caused Adam and Eve to use fig leaves to hide from God in the garden. It was totally their mindset and belief. None of it came from God, but it was very real to them because of their ability to now 'discern' what was good or bad apart from God.

Beloved, we cannot afford to walk in that pattern of offence. Once that mindset is embraced, fig leaves are created and they are placed over our Light and true ability in Christ. If we are not conscious we will hide behind the nature of this fallen understanding and place more attention on darkness, than we do His ability. This turns ministry opportunities into personal physical battles when they were never intended to be so. The adversary's favorite tactic is making our battles seem personal and physical. He knows he cannot win if we understand who we are and what is in us. David knew that there was more in him and more with him going up against a seasoned giant of war. This understanding provided him victory while saving his people from national shame. We too experience great victory when we operate outside of our ability and allow the greater Light in us to come forward.

We will journey into what this same Light that is working on the inside of you truly looks like. What does a giant killer or someone actually operating in their recreated spirit look and act like? This is our goal. By the time you finish the last chapter, I believe there will be a mentality shift that will cause both the churched and the unchurched to experience the Father's heart through you with greater impact. The lost are really in darkness and only a Light that is reprogrammed will be able to reach many of those in need.

Allow this reading to encourage you on the inside. When you have the mind of Christ, what seems abundantly evident to the masses, will not necessarily be true for you. This really is a mentality shift on many different levels of relationship. *How will I navigate when darkness is attempting to overshadow the mentality of Christ within? How will I respond to those around me still accommodating the fig leaf fallen nature? Am I willing to take the Word for what it says? Am I willing to shift my thinking in order to maximize the impact of the Light of Christ within?* We will seek to practically walk as Light and Love, nothing more - nothing less.

Let us not allow anyone to rob our candlestick. We cannot permit fig leaves to hide the brightness of the Light of Christ and still experience victory. Rise up and declare that you will no longer allow the enemy to offer the dark sides of a fallen nature to take preeminence over your witness. Beloved, only by this Light will they know you are His disciples. Let us change the present mentality of accommodating fig leaves, and be emboldened to walk in the Light of Truth.

2

the Present Mentality

The present mentality of most believers has unfortunately accepted the fact that a world where unconditional Love is purely given and experienced with others regardless of race, sex or creed is more utopia than something we should consider normal. While we acknowledge that walking in unconditional Love can be ideal, we also understand it presents a daring and complicated journey that most are not ready to add to an overflowing plate. As divorce rates rise, sex appeal sells, and casual eroticism becomes the socially accepted norm, we are subconsciously bombarded with schools of thought that run contrary to who we were created to be. In fact, modern culture can be so overwhelmingly convincing that even those created to be the Light in a dark world have begun to doubt the sanctity of the lifestyle of Love.

We all deal with darkness and experience its effects on the decisions we make every day. Even a child raised in a faith based home from birth, will experience darkness either firsthand or vicariously through outlets of social media. No matter how pure our background or upbringing, we must be conscious to reprogram what we are experiencing on a daily basis. For when we are not conscious, the mind begins to subconsciously embrace everything we are experiencing around us as 'truth'. This truth is constructed by everything seen by our eyes, heard through our ears and includes fictional situations viewed in media, reality television shows and others experiences witnessed in the lives of our peers. Whether bad or good, these experiences all work together to shape our reality and they influence the decisions we make on our desired style of dress, how we communicate and ultimately determine how we handle personal interactions with the opposite sex. If we are not conscious to reprogram, our perception of what is true will slowly begin to mimic an increasingly sensual culture of influence. This culture measures 'good' by thoughts and feelings, or by how something or someone makes us feel. This type of secular thinking clearly runs opposite of the mind of Christ and the nature of unconditional Love.

Has the salt of the earth lost its seasoning?

When we face any circumstance with a secular mindset, walking in the Light of Christ becomes extremely difficult. We may honestly endeavor to walk upright and live in purity, but it is impossible to walk in true purity if the mind has not been consciously reprogrammed of what we are experiencing around us. Everything we allow on the computer screens of our mind creates a form of reality in our heart. So as we begin to embrace the reality of what we see around us as 'truth', quite frankly - we lose seasoning. We lose the ability to walk as the Light of Christ and experience the victory that everything His nature affords us. We are in essence exchanging what we are supposed to be – life, for what secular experience is offering – death.

This is why many believers may walk out of the shadows of immorality, but continue to operate from an imbalanced mindset when it comes to Love, sexuality and depth of relationship with the opposite sex. As a renewed spirit the promiscuity of the past may no longer be desired at heart, but without conscious reprogramming of mind, any interaction with the opposite sex will be heavily influenced by the secular culture experienced every day. This culture embraces the erotic language of love that controls the nature of how the secular mind interacts with the opposite sex. This causes a mental struggle between what the recreated spirit desires – positive intimacy and influence, versus what culture consistently proposes as reality to the mind.

Eventually through much prayer, fasting and sacrifice we may breakthrough cultural influence and find peace of mind. However, without conscious reprogramming, it will be extremely difficult since the battlefield of what the heart embraces as truth starts within our thoughts. This is why we are instructed in Romans to reprogram the thought life of our mind. *Do not be conformed to this world, but be transformed by the renewing of your mind. Then you will be able to discern what is the good, pleasing, and perfect will of God. – Romans 12:2*

Without conscious reprogramming, our secular experiences will define what is good, and socially acceptable.   This presents an ongoing struggle. For instance, many of us have found Christ after living lifestyles that were not healthy to our destiny or the lives around us. To be honest, it is inevitable. Our flesh is inclined to do whatever it likes, wants and desires. Starting at birth, the attributes of the flesh are present and naturally desirous of anything it feels will bring contentment.

The bible describes the characteristics of flesh in Galatians 5:19-21, e.g., *adultery, fornication, dirtiness, idolatry, profanity, witchcraft, wizardry, hatred, arguments, distrust, rage, selfish ambition, conflicts, heresies, envy, murder, drunkenness, revelries.* Written down, they are blatant negative attributes, but when presented through the medium of entertainment on film, glorified through music and viewed through social media, they are much more palatable or even desirable.   When the works of the flesh are experienced through media, by default we naturally begin to aspire to lifestyles that may not equal what we initially embraced as good or acceptable. Our life experiences continue to feed the mind until it becomes a product of the surrounding secular culture.

However, when we consciously reprogram our minds according to Romans 12:2, we understand that our cultural ways of thinking are not always His way of thinking, and oftentimes runs polar opposite. Though certain lifestyles may be socially acceptable for the masses, it may not be acceptable for us as viewed from a renewed mind. This understanding outlines the difference between the believing *conscious* mind and the secular <u>subconscious</u> mind. The conscious mind is in constant communication with the nature of Christ within. This believer is led irrespective of actual circumstance and popular opinion. To walk in this dimension, you must have more value in the position of your candlestick, than you do with being in line with social acceptance.

Unfortunately, tradition has helped define the mind of Christ as being some abstract form of self-denial and the limitation of anything pleasing. While we cannot discount the fact that there is significant self-denial involved in conscious thought, we must come to realization that there is an unhealthy imbalance placed on limitation, and discover what the Father has for us on the other side.

For instance, as a believer it is consistently heard that, "You cannot do this! - You are restricted from that... and stay away from this!" Many books have been written about what this list entails and how we can find peace within these limitations. However, the instructions given to those who have the mind of Christ were given to season the lives of others, and to provide a liberty that is a natural part of our recreated transformation. We are referenced to Light and salt many times throughout scripture. We are encouraged to esteem others higher than ourselves and share a Love with others that will break chains. However, when our mind is operating under the influence of a secular culture, we suppress our Light and embrace the constraints of limitations that fail to bring honor to God. Furthermore, the limitations we place on the Light of Christ within do not come from any examples in scripture, in actuality we see Christ and other leaders operating totally outside the boundaries and limitations of the fleshly fallen nature.

Everything about our make-up was created for His glory. We were all given an eternal 'Light of the world' that came with an embedded command to outwardly shine. We also have a recreated spirit that is completely contrary to darkness. Again, everything about us is desirous to walk worthy of our heavenly dimension. However, while these parts of our make-up may possess the ability, command and desire to shine, we still need to renew our mind to allow us to walk in practical application. A mind that has not been consciously reprogrammed will find it easier to simply avoid anything that remotely resembles the very 'shadow' of darkness. However, the purpose of the Light is not to remain hidden or introverted from the world. Oftentimes what we are judging as darkness or dangerous has not been labelled that by God. We are simply using our fallen nature to navigate a dominion that was given supernaturally and must be maintained supernaturally. At no point are we ever asked to use secular judgments to protect the Light within. We are instructed to maintain the good thing committed to us by the Holy Ghost (*2 Timothy 1:14*). This means we are always operating by the dictates of supernatural instruction. We are never called to subject our Light and abilities to fallen man in scripture, but contrariwise, we are encouraged to place it where those can see. Those of the fallen nature, who are in darkness, are those who need the Light the most. ***"No one lights a lamp and puts it in a place where it will be hidden, or under a bowl. Instead they put it on its stand, so that those who come in may see the light." ~ Luke 11:33***

We are encouraged to shine and be the thermostat by which our surroundings align to. If we are reactive to the darkness around us, we will find that the power of darkness will be unknowingly magnified over the power of the Light of Christ.

We walk right by, and talk directly to ministry opportunities every day, but because the secular mind is in operation promoting fear; the fear of lust, fear of manipulation, fear of physical attraction or fear of repulsion or rejection, <u>we miss them</u>. Most of us have failed to realize that this type of thinking places us in direct conflict with scripture that says, ***"Ye are the light of the world. A city that is set on a hill cannot be hid. 15 Neither do men light a candle, and put it under a bushel, but on a candlestick; and it gives light unto <u>all</u> that are in the house." - Matthew 5:14-15.***

There is great darkness on the world, and we are called to be the Light to those lost in that darkness. We are instructed to place our Light on a candlestick so the effectiveness of it can be known, not kept hidden. Instead, we often cower behind modernism, new human rights, and a thought process of social acceptance that only dampens our shine. There is no difference between unknowingly walking behind a culture that is blocking our Light, or willfully hiding the Light. The end result of both scenarios is that those in darkness never benefit from the Light of Christ within.

Contrary to culture, my wife and I have consciously chosen to be deliberate in understanding the value of the candlestick, champion original biblical instruction concerning our Light and act on what we believe in our everyday relationships.

With most of secular society bending towards sexualization and following the fleshly passion, we have found the easiest place to be conscious of our Light shining Love walk has been demonstrating it through our interactions with those of the opposite sex. Of course, this has been misconstrued many times by our friends and relatives and many "brothers and sisters" on the outside looking in. Honestly, most of them have never experienced positive intimacy with the opposite gender - ever. Any intimate thought or close relationship that involved someone of the opposite sex was experienced largely through an erotic love language. In addition to those personal experiences, 99% of intimate interaction seen in film, heard in music and experienced through the life of their peers also spoke the same erotic love language. So subconsciously, the reality of any interaction with the opposite sex deeper than a surface greeting carried some form of erotic end game and was now looked at with mal-intentions.

Some of us have simply accepted that the language of Love is universally erotic. We have settled here, and so guard our heart and try and to get as much as we can within what our limitations allow, but ultimately, we have resolved to believe there is no Utopia of Agape Love. This is why for most women, a hug no longer feels like a protective embrace from a brother who Loves them and feels a responsibility for them. To this day in our churches all across the globe, a simple hug has become a battlefield of emotion and distrust, and starts a gauntlet of vulnerable possibilities that we altogether have decided to simply avoid. As a result, in the place that should be known for acceptance and unconditional Love, you will oftentimes receive the 'church hug' salutation. This is the lukewarm partial embrace received from church goers that is more politician than Christian as it seeks to protect the Light from the darkness of sin.

We have essentially surrendered the battle of Love to eroticism, and instead of leading the way and teaching the world the difficult language of the narrow path of Agape by first understanding the proper characteristics of unconditional Love, we have in turn chosen to consciously acknowledge darkness first and 'protect' our Lights from its shade. This is unbiblical and certainly not Christ like. It damages our vulnerability and discourages connections that the Father has actually created for our good. When we do not understand our roles in the lives of one another, we sabotage our own progressions.

It is not possible to efficiently move forward in destiny without properly connecting with those who are ordained to be a part of our lives. So when we immediately discount possible connections with someone of the opposite gender as evil or fleshly, not taking into consideration the purity of

Agape connection, we not only potentially abort missing links to our destiny but we now limit the scope of those we can partner with to one gender; and for some, one gender and one ethnicity or creed. This mentality has not only stifled the proliferation of our Faith but it continues to be a stumbling block in the lives of many others across the globe. For how can we progress in Light while viewing everything through the spectacles of darkness? We simply cannot properly see the road or assignments ahead when looking through this filter, and unfortunately, we will continue to walk in darkness until the present mentality changes, one mind at a time.

SO HOW DO WE CHANGE OUR MIND?

Changing this mindset can be a daunting task, largely because of our inclination to identify darkness before we allow our Light an opportunity to be effective. When we are so inclined to practice a posture of defensive withdrawal, we can lose sight of our responsibilities to be the Light of the world. This wisdom of 'holy introversion' is largely the result of a modern viewpoint of scripture. The most popular coming from, *1 Thessalonians 5: 22 "Abstain from every form of Evil"*, and other versions of the scripture that say, *"Abstain from the very appearance of Evil"*. But this scripture was not given to us for bondage or to encourage us to remove our Light from its candlestick. However, we will oftentimes find restrictions being placed on our Light simply because of what a natural minded onlooker may think.

Paul explains in *1 Corinthians 2:14-16 "the natural man does not receive the things of the Spirit of God for they are foolishness to him; nor can he know them, because they are spiritually discerned. But he who is spiritual judges all things,* **yet he himself is rightly judged by no one.** *For who has known the mind of the Lord that he may instruct Him? But* **we** *have the* **mind of Christ.** *"* We are actually encouraged to avoid any sort of holy introversion that will cause us to hide our Light in Christ as a result of the judgments of darkness. Those operating in a natural mind oftentimes will not know how to properly discern what Light is.

In *Titus 1:15,* we see that *"to the pure all things are pure, but to the defiled and disbelieving all things are defiled."* These are plain truths in scripture that encourage us to boldly walk in the Light regardless of what secular minded individuals and cultures may think.

We cannot know these truths and then stand idle and allow darkness to judge our Light and dictate how we interact with those around us. This is our mission field and operating in Love is the language that speaks and communicates the loudest and clearest. We must be emboldened to proactively walk in the character of God no matter how foolish we may seem to outsiders of a natural mind.   Think of this, if most decisions we make are under the influence of something greater than our flesh and natural mind, how then can we subject ourselves to the natural minded judgment of others who live and judge from the vantage point of flesh? This simply will not render effective ministry. Oftentimes, the strongest leaders and spiritually minded individuals may not really understand the 'Why' of everything they do.   It is impossible, and frankly it would not be considered faith if they logically understood everything they were called to do. We are not always able to explain what the Father is leading us to do but we know our obedience is supported by His word through scripture.

Again, we were never instructed to have our actions supported by the secularly minded.   As scripture states, spiritual things simply look foolish and "evil" in the sight of the natural mind. Most times when we fall short, it is at the place where we decide which voice to listen to. Flesh or Spirit. Supernatural or Natural. Both are competing for their will to be done, but only one can win. When we look at the life of Jesus, we see the main difference between us and this perfect man was His choice to never allow darkness to change His stance.   He heard the voice of two opinions, yet He chose to not react and He listened to the leading of the Spirit no matter how great the cost. We must consciously choose to listen to the Spirit of God while a conforming and culturally accepted school of thought is vying for our ear. If we fail to do this, we will never learn the language of Agape and our Lights will remain hidden to those who need it most. Decide to change this mentality today. Vow to understand the nature of Christ and how you can effectively shine your Light regardless of how loud the judgments from the world around you may be. With this understanding you will find effective and life transforming ministry that opens the eyes of the blind and heals the hidden and imbalanced places of the heart.

3

Proactive Vs. Reactive

One of the greatest attributes of Jesus was that He *never* reacted to anyone or any situation, but instead He pro-acted - from His spirit. The actions recorded of His life came from the knowledge of who HE was and the understanding of His purpose. He did not simply respond to circumstances. He consciously took action based on who, and who was inside Him. He said, *"...Truly, truly, I tell you, the Son can do nothing by Himself, unless He sees the Father doing it. For whatever the Father does, the Son also does." John 5:19*

The actions we see Jesus take were not simply responses to what He was experiencing, but a conscious pro-action of who He was. Part of the journey to live as Christ is learning how not to simply react in response to an event or experience. We must understand our purpose and take action based on the understanding of who we are and what is in us or we will find defeat lurking around the corner of every experience.

As a youth I had a lot of sleepovers with friends that resulted in many late nights in which we would play lots of tricks, daring one another to do some pretty curious and downright hysterical things. At these sleep overs you never wanted to be the first one to doze off because someone always had a plan to make the group laugh at your expense. I can name quite a few tricks we played over the years but the most common was the shaving cream or toothpaste game. The idea was to place one of these substances in the hand while someone else would either tickle the nose or prick the eye to get you to bring your hand up as fast as you could, and since the victim was asleep he was unaware that he was slapping away the nuisance from his face with a handful of shaving cream or globs of toothpaste. So when their hand met the face with force, or if the victim would screamed as the toothpaste began to irritate the eye, we would all laugh ourselves silly. We could create these humorous situations for ourselves simply because we knew how one would react. Some reacted violently, hitting themselves so hard that shaving cream would splatter everywhere. At that time, it was a funny adolescent treat, but to this day it still teaches a lesson on predictable subconscious responses.

When we are reactive, we give our adversary the advantage of knowing exactly what our response will be to situations or temptations that he creates for us. When our subconscious is the decision maker, it has not been properly submitted to higher levels of thinking and is so is subjected to reacting to the whims of the flesh. We may think we are acting from faith, but this is not always true. Unless we have given Light an opportunity to voice its wisdom and shine in the dark places, we are simply reacting. This reactive nature of action gives our adversary the ability to predetermine our future by leading us down pathways to which our responses are predictable and subconscious. Essentially, we become a puppet inevitably losing control of our destiny. Much like the victims of the childhood shaving cream prank, our enemy will be laughing at our reactions and decision making, while we are left cleaning up the mess.

We cannot afford to be reactionary at this stage of present darkness. Most of us sense this and are actively searching for the understanding of the narrow way. Even by reading this book you are seeking a higher form of thought, but we must renew our minds to understand how to pro-act in every situation. We cannot expect success in fulfilling the destiny of our assignment if we are allowing our belief system to be shaped by low level thought processes. The Bible tells us that Jesus also felt the negative effects of lower levels of thought and was tempted in every way that we are tempted and ever will be. Meaning our savior saw exactly what you and I see, but the reason He was a perfect man is because He consistently chose to *pro-act* based upon His Spirit. He chose to be consciously aware of His Spirit at all times and He gave to others according to His higher process of thought, not according to their dark systems of belief. Proactive thinkers are always in character. We must adamantly choose to make decisions based on shining the Light of Christ regardless of how much you may be demonized or ridiculed by the social majority. Al Hollingsworth, a great teacher and mentor once told me, "To be successful, it requires that you master your emotions..." In these modern times of moral depravity, this statement speaks volumes. To be proactive we must learn to rule well our surroundings and consciously monitor what is allowed entrance into the computer of our mind. Everything we see, hear, taste and touch all create experiences that bear witness to the reality of some belief system that will control the destiny of our life. And so when we fail to consciously feed our experiences the thoughts we want to become, we ultimately become a product of the environment and simply react to the whims of circumstance. Success requires that we master our emotions, possess the power of will, and continue to press towards a mark outside the boundary of what is seen around us. If true success, true Love, happiness and wealth came by simply meeting someone in a daily routine and thinking like everyone else thinks, then the majority population would be successful, content and wealthy. However, that is not the case. Most of the world has become a product of mass media. We hear what the radio wants us to hear and see what the major networks want us to see and go pay even more money to view movies that theatres have predicted the majority of us will like. Everything we deem 'good' is created by social acceptance and judgments of the environment around us. As our lives will attest, failure to operate consciously causes us to simply fall victim to the norm. The end result of these choices greatly dampen our ability to experience effective ministry and positive intimacy.

Modern convenience and the desire to be comfortable at all times actually keeps us from that which we truly desire. Most of us want great relationships with people and truly desire to walk in positive intimacy with others, but if we never do anything other than the socially accepted 'norm', we will never really experience the true character of others. We must choose progress. Again, we cannot react to darkness the same way as the masses and expect to complete divine assignments. When the higher thought process is rejected, we not only damage our lives but we remove the opportunity for others to reprogram their future actions as well.

Oftentimes, the Father desires to use the Light in us to show someone a way of escape. Not everyone wants to live in sin. Many of them are looking for a different way. Searching for a better way out but do not know what that out looks like. Many men only know womanizing and adultery. While many women have been trained to manipulate their bodies and 'use what God gave you' to get ahead. For these, our brothers and sisters, there is limited hope unless they experience something other than Reaction and Holy Introversion. Jesus consciously chose not to react. He did not take offense, react or become introverted simply because of the sin of someone else or their lack of spiritual aura. Again, Jesus exemplified how to pro-act from the Life in us and never react to the darkness of the world around us.

FOR WHAT GOOD IS A PHYSICIAN TO THOSE ALREADY HEALED?

Jesus was able to minister to the tax collectors, thieves, pimps and prostitutes of His day because He was proactive in every situation. This is the reason His ministry was so effective and culturally shocking. I am certain that some of the harlots of the day approached Jesus with their coquettish tones. I can imagine them saying, "Hey Daddy, what can I do for you?"

You know... harlot linguistics.

Now, maybe Jesus, whom was tempted in all points (in every way) we are, yet without sin (Hebrews 4:15), was probably taken aback at first. He most certainly knew exactly where this woman was coming from, but still He chose not to **react** to her darkness and fleshly nature. No, He knew this would shut her off from His source of living water, so He chose to PRO-ACT from His internal spirit connection to the Father. He chose to pro-act in obedience to the Father despite the sinful soul that was before His presence. He did not tuck and run hoping to dodge the religious paparazzi so that no one would see the likes of His anointing interacting with the local prostitute. And He certainly did not separate Himself from her darkened state in efforts to save His anointing. On the contrary, Jesus actually esteemed her salvation higher than His position or status. I have yet to find any indication in scripture where our Father will judge you for esteeming a pimp, prostitute, liar, homosexual, greedy person, stripper or robber higher than yourself. Nothing we ever read in scripture will condemn us for freely sharing the Light of Christ to those in darkness. Again, Jesus pro-acted and left the perfect example of how effective ministry can be when we walk in the Love of God and consider those in darkness before ourselves.

A story of Proactive ministry:

As a teenager and young adult I was heavily involved in music ministry. I would often perform concerts for charities, churches and schools in my local area. Almost any place I could grab a mic and grace a stage to get the ear of the youth captivated by my gifts, I was there, and performing. This sometimes brought me to places that most would fear to go. Once I held a Unity Concert in a very urban area in Los Angeles to bring peace between two rival gang factions. Looking back, these were exactly the places that needed what was in me most. Not many were willing to travel past drug dealers, prostitutes and gang members to simply perform an act that was not always received. Oftentimes we were met with disdain by those not wanting to be awaken and that was not always appealing, but we were on assignment. One night in particular, I was leaving an event held in a local theatre in an urban area of Los Angeles called Inglewood. Coming fresh off the stage, I felt great. I ministered in song amongst other saved peers and was well received. Many were touched and greeted me after the performance saying how blessed they were by my gift. So naturally my Spirit was highly encouraged. As I was driving away from the venue, I noticed a lady on the corner of that street and the next block. She had all the appearances of a prostitute and soon beckoned for my attention as I approached to make a turn at the corner. I slowed my car and rolled my window down. At this point, most people I tell this story to say. "You did what?" *Yes, I slowed my car and rolled my window down. Admittedly, even I was afraid of my witness and the appearance of 'the minister's' car stopping at a corner and speaking to a lady, or rather, engaging an alleged prostitute. No matter which way you look at this picture, in the eyes of the world or the eyes of those stooped in the mindset of reactionary thinking, "guilty" would be my verdict. If I were to be placed on trial, the arresting officer could just play the video of me getting into my car, slowing down at the corner, rolling my window down and engaging a woman that everyone would rightfully classify as a prostitute. And to be frank, she was. But again, as the Holy Spirit began to change my mind about women over the years, she now was no longer a threat to me or my anointing, no matter how tight her dress and how long her legs. According to scripture, she was my sister and according to Jesus, I needed to pro-act in Faith and be led by my light and not react to her darkness. My spirit simply wanted to know her state, and if I could offer her a way out, I would. After rolling my window down, I spoke first. "Hey Sis, how are you doing?" She almost immediately began to cry. She begged for my help. Honestly at first, I thought she was a set up. At the time, I was in Real Estate and drove a pretty decent car and so my reaction was that she knew I had something of worth to take. 'Don't be stupid" I heard. "She is playing you. You see this car. What does this look like? You just left the stage. Anybody coming out will see you and what will Christ look like then? Leave her alone!" But again, we are called to esteem others higher than ourselves and we are called to pro-act not react to circumstance and I was getting a firsthand lesson in what this meant. She explained to me that she only needed a ride to the bus station. I obliged and opened the door for her to get in. Believe me, at this point, the enemy is doing all he can in my mind to stop this interaction, but all the while I am fighting to remain conscious of the voice of the Holy Spirit. She thanked me and explained in horrific detail how she was just physically abused and needed to get out of the business. A few minutes into our ride I learned how, just a few minutes prior, another gentleman kicked her out of his car after she rejected to give him a sexual favor for his kind act. This lady was in a very broken place. She was freshly beaten. Emotionally degraded. Oppressed and mentally abused. All she knew was the street corner and because of this she needed to be met on the same street corner to receive help. It was almost 11pm and not many churches were open at that time, especially in that area. For her, there really was no way of escape from this situation at that hour and in that particular place. No way of escape, except the Christ in me. (It is the same Light that dwells in you).*

I often look back at this and sense how deeply the Father is pleading for a generation to change our way of thinking. If we do not change our reactive lower level thought process, God will never have anyone to use in a similar situation. Even if she actually prayed for help, who would be there to help her? Would you? Are you available to consciously hear the voice of the Holy Spirit in similar circumstances? Consider the situation. Without knowing the background or end result of this altercation, are you prepared to pro-act in this way? If not, what type of help can she depend on at that street corner, at that hour and dressed in those clothes? When we arrived at the bus station, I paid for her bus ticket, prayed with her, blessed her and sent her on her way feeling worthy, loved and valued. The Holy Spirit had just used me to plant a seed that could be watered to bring even more increase at another time in her future. After telling her she was loved and needed to reunite with her family in the place she was traveling, she responded like I was Jesus and had just giving her new life. Overjoyed and thankful, she knew God met her that night in the form of a young man who was learning to be less reactive and more like Christ. Beloved, let us all learn how to Love one another.

4

Lower Level Thinking (LLT)

Unlike modern adolescent thinking, it was cool to be different and somewhat unique growing up. In the 80's and 90's we enjoyed marketing campaigns and slogans that said, "Dare to be different". In churches you would often hear preachers saying, "Be Different" and "Enter through the Narrow Gate!" "For wide is the road that leads to destruction but narrow is the path that leads to righteousness and few find it!"

You too have most likely heard this passage of scripture from Luke 7:13 several times. But, what does the wide road of destruction look like? Or, what about the narrow path? How narrow is it, and why is there only a few that find it?

This can be quite disturbing when you seek to be obedient but find it difficult since everyone around you is riding along on the same road. Who will be there to tell you if the road you are traveling on is indeed the wide road of destruction if everyone is following the same cookie cutter patterns? Who is to say it is the wide road or narrow road? How am I to know if my path is the narrow path? Or if I am one of the few that have found it? The wide road of destruction is indeed very wide, very accommodating and heavily traveled largely because it is so easy to navigate, convenient for just about everything and highly desired by the physical senses.

Most would agree it is quite natural to do whatever brings comfort and convenience to our bodies. In our modern era, fast food chains and pharmaceutical companies are making billions of dollars catering to the lifestyle of convenience. Though we now understand that the long term effects of living for convenience and fast-food diet plans may not be the best standard of living, it still has not changed the mind of the masses concerning dietary convenience. Additionally, most espouse beliefs that say anything that seems right to do and does not offend others is generally a safe bet. This thinking far outgrows our dietary choices and has trickled into the philosophy of our lifestyles. However, if we are to believe scripture and desire the narrow path, we discover that this thinking is completely backwards and flat out wrong, no matter what is widely accepted by the masses.

We consider it entertaining when we give our attention to shows and videos that we know are made strictly for an appetite of flesh. Whether it be violence, sexuality, profanity, greed or vanity, we really have no problem giving it our attention, and paying to do so. As long as it is acceptable to major production studios, news outlets and peers, it becomes easier to embrace as acceptable.

The general populace desires many forms of fleshly convenience and prides itself on tolerance of just about anything as long as there is no harm done to another being or animal. A wide road of human rights has overridden the palate for what is scriptural and blurred the boundary lines of right and wrong. We see the same popular mindset play out over and over again in the lives of celebrities, leaders, politicians, parents and peers but we have not correlated the reasons why many are experiencing a common end.

We may ask, "How is this **not** acceptable behavior if *everyone* eats this way, *everyone* acts this way, *everyone* interacts with the opposite sex this way, dresses this way, hugs this way, watches these sorts of movies and talks this way?" The list of what we witness *everyone* else doing can be unending, but the outside world has never been the measuring stick for the Light. Essentially, we are unknowingly accepting the experiences of our surroundings as truth, while the purpose of our Light is put aside. This, in fact, is the experience of the wide road of destruction.

The Bible says that our Faith, or *our belief system*, is created and built on what we hear – Romans 10:17. So as we live out our day to day lives, our belief system and levels of faith are being spoon fed to us, subconsciously. Think about every commercial, cinematic feature film, favorite song or TV show and what it is actually creating inside of you. As we give our attentions to these things that are happening around us, our reality and belief system is being formed (or conformed) whether we approve of the message or not. Just like we tend to pick up certain accents, slang and sayings just based on what we hear and experience around us; we also develop our belief systems and faith for what we expectancy in life based on what we are giving our attention to. If we are to walk the narrow road, it must be a conscious journey that requires effort and the mind of Christ.

When we choose to go along with the masses we lose the mind of Christ and inherit a reaction based mindset. This thought process thinks like the world, reacts to circumstance and desires socially acceptable practices. Most of the world is responsive to this lower level subconscious thought pattern. Our goal will be to avoid this trap as much as possible and enter a realm of higher thinking where destiny will be fulfilled and ministry to others will be magnified.

Lower Level Thought (LLT) process consists of:

- A Mindset that is formed by **earthly** experiences
- A Thought pattern that is a product of **practices acceptable to the masses**
- A Mindset built on **convenience** and what I need for **comfort**

- A Thought pattern that allows **fleshly desire** and **cultural experiences** to shape and define reality
- A Mindset that is **contrary to the Mind of Christ** and Word of God
- A Thought pattern that is highly REACTIVE in nature

The LLT process is a subtle and convenient mindset that is extremely destructive to the nature and character of Christ. The nature of Light is always shining forth in conscious action. It draws its energy from sources outside of this world in which we can see, while LLT draws from the validation of man and things of this world. One of the reasons the secular world dares not join 'the church' is because they see these people who are supposed to represent Light, but they are doing the same things that the world knows are wrong (dark). The bible says that even a child knows what is pure and what is Light (Proverbs 20:11), so certainly the secular mind knows what is Light and what is not. We are fooling no one when we do everything the secular world does, and show that we think just like the secular world thinks. Yet, we still find a way to profess to be different and somehow deserving of heaven while our counterparties are condemned to eternal hell fire.

Without being conscious of our purpose, the LLT process causes us to forfeit the power of our witness that naturally accompanies walking in the Light. This is why it is very important that we pay conscious attention to what the Light is created to do, and less on what the enemy is doing. The enemy is always present to counterfeit the higher assignment of Light through *emotion*, what we think we understand with our *natural logic*, and *lower level thought* (**LLT**). And when we decide to stop at the lower level thoughts or "counterfeit" feelings, it is at this point we choose to abort the higher calling of our assignment and miss out on the true ministry of fulfilling a purpose greater than ourselves. In practicality, let us consider the following example of a meeting between a woman and a man for the very first time.

A woman is out around town going about her normal routine running her errands. While she is shopping minding her own affairs she comes in contact with many people. A service man who changes the oil on her car, the mailman, her favorite teller at the bank, the wait staff at the neighborhood diner and others. They all meet her acquaintance at some point throughout the day. One day, the service man who changes the oil on her car has a longer than usual conversation with her. It is a good conversation but she senses that there is an attraction to her (Eros), and/or she is in some small way drawn to him. As a result of this 'attraction' that she perceives is negative and fleshly, she aborts any further action, conversation or thought because she desires to keep herself Pure (Holy). Flesh has been aborted and ministry has been protected.

... Or, has it?

Here, is good place to exchange natural (LLT) logic for higher thinking. Why do we make decisions based on low level negativity? And why do most interactions stop here, at this negative perception? No ministry has taken place. No Light has been shown, and thus far, only darkness has had a voice. Only someone speaking a different Love language (Agape) and operating in a higher consciousness (Mind of Christ) can actually identify the truth and provide a corrective course of action. When we began to correct our perceptions and remove flesh from the principal seat of 'attraction', generational cycles of improper manipulation and flirtation can be broken.

For example:

With an understanding of Agape Love and who she is in Christ (the Light of the world), this exchange could provide many different facets of ministry. The Light of Christ shines in the darkest places and gives life to dead situations. With the audience of this gentleman's life, any word from God spoken to him would be received. His marriage could be encouraged, day brightened and any fruit of the Spirit you choose could be imparted. But any impartation will only happen with an individual operating in a higher thought life. When we operate with the same caliber lower level thought life of the world, we hide the Light of Christ and diminish our impact. However, once we give Light the principle seat of attention, generational cycles of improper manipulation and flesh can be broken.

This may not work perfectly in every situation, but at least we can allow the Light an opportunity to shine before we make decisions based solely on the fear of darkness. Oftentimes, we are the only Light people will see. The only Jesus they will interact with and we are running lost in the fields of lower level thinking.

Women should not introvert the Light of Christ simply because of the lower level thoughts experienced around men. If this happens, how will men ever have an opportunity to break the cycle of lower level thinking? Most men cannot comprehend what a conversation with a virtuous woman with a higher thought life sounds like because so many women are programmed to protect their virtue through introversion. On the other hand, most women today will not know what a man of God looks like because very few men have been properly taught how to surrender their actions to a higher thought process. Moreover, the men who are happily married in monogamy will sense the same attraction, and like the women, walk in introversion. Oftentimes, the actions we take to 'protect' ourselves and improperly react to daily situations, are actually hiding our Lights from those who need it most. This form of introversion is strictly reactionary, it is without biblical precedent and dangerously treads in the waters of self-righteous.

As carriers of Light, we cannot continue to make decisions based solely on darkness. We must begin to pro-act in Light and operate from a higher plane of thought. If we fail to change our thinking to a higher thought process, we will create environments that shun the lost and hide our Lights. We are essentially requiring the lost to present themselves as fully healed to even hold a meaningful conversation. Jesus never hid His Light in such a way. He looked for opportunities to witness to those in darkness whether He was interacting with a harlot, a woman at a well, possessed naked man or else. It is as if we are now requiring those in darkness to earn an opportunity to speak with the Light. The Light of Christ should always be looking for ways to engage others and esteem them higher than our natural judgments so that **He** may have an audience with them in some way. This is one reason why the Gospel message does not look like the Good News today. Our Light has lost its luster, and our mantra to "Be Different" has been replaced with goals of inclusion and carries desires to be just like everyone else. We do not want to be considered different. We want to watch the same things others do, talk like others do and be esteemed like others do. We have swallowed whole the lower level thought trap of our enemy - hook, line and sinker. If we desire to operate in Agape

Love, we should be proactively looking for places to let our Light shine. When we refuse to shine our Light, it is only hidden to those that are lost and need it most.

The lower level love language of the world is very poisonous and is affecting our marriages, our healing and our witness. Part of our witness is how we serve the broken, but we cannot service them when we require those in need of the healing to come 'looking' like the healed. It can be cringe worthy when you listen to believers as they talk about how they employ methods of introversion and how far they go to 'protect the anointing' in this modern society. We go on to confirm our stances of introversion by rehearsing how we are 'a virtuous woman' or 'man of valor and prestige' and will not be seen mingling with the likes of darkness. We must remember that those in darkness, need the Light of the gospel the most. If our Light is hid, it is hid from those who need it most *(2 Corinthians 4:3)*. We cannot place judgments on the Light because of the darkness of the world. Again, we are called to sinners. We are called to the lost and broken. We are not called to go in the opposite direction because we carry Light and they live in the dark. That does not represent the Kingdom of Heaven.

To be honest, the desires of introversion is largely reminiscent of the spirit that influenced the disciples as Jesus attempted to minister to the lost. When the disciples found Jesus mingling amongst the harlotry and tax collectors, they could not believe a man carrying such a Light like Jesus had would hang around such a lowly group. Jesus immediately corrected them. He told them that they needed to be mindful that these people were exactly who needed the Light the most (Luke 5:27-31, Mark 2:15-17). He was a physician that came to set free. The broken and lowly are the ones who need the great physician the most.

We were likewise found in our sin. Who reading this book came to the Light already bearing your own? We all were in need of a savior. A physician that could locate us in our sin, show us the way, and exchange our fallen nature for His Spirit. We need to extend the same invitation to those currently in darkness. When did we start to agree with the reaction of the disciples' lower lever thought (LLT) about those around Jesus?

These interactions happen around us every day, and we can choose to either react to the perceived darkness others or allow the Light of Christ to shine though us. For what need is there of a physician if the physician will only engage those who are already healed, or appear non-threatening? The enemy cunningly created this mindset, and if we continue to operate in the lower level thought (LLT) process we are severely limiting our impact. He knows this, and is content with our introversion. If you believe that because of your Light you must refrain from those in darkness, Satan himself will confirm you and begin to tell you, "You know what, you are the biggest light in the city". If that is all it takes to keep the Light of Christ in you hidden from those he desires to keep in darkness, you may receive confirmation from corner of the earth.

Our adversary is a master deceiver. We must adopt a higher mindset and learn to operate from heaven in our daily interactions. You are the bright Light in a dark world. Reprogram your thought life to let your Light shine. Beloved, stay far away from the LLT process and let your Light shine!

5

Counterfeit Feelings

We are truly deceiving ourselves and *SEVERELY LIMITING* the higher thought process of Christ if we continue to fail in recognizing fleshly reactions as flesh and nothing more than <u>counterfeit</u> feelings that distract us from fulfilling our assignment. Much like in the previous story of the lady on the street corner, our assignments are contrary to secular opinion and completely spiritual in nature. We will oftentimes need to consider not the things which are seen because the things which we see are temporary, but the things which we do not see, are truth (*II Corinthians 4:18*). Through the lens of Christ, the prostitute lifestyle I saw the lady on the corner leading was only temporary. What I did not see with my natural eye was her eternal destiny. That is why we never judge by what we can see in the natural (that is temporary), but we are instructed to look at what cannot be seen with the natural eye (eternal purpose and destiny in Christ). No one can look at you with the natural eye and see your eternal destiny. They will only see a snapshot of a temporary position. In the same manner, if we are going to carry a life giving Spirit inside of us, we need to train ourselves to not judge with our eyes and act based on our purpose (give life/shine Light). However, we do not always adhere to that scripture. We must daily strive to see others through the eyes of Christ and not allow our lower level thoughts to dictate how we interact.

I am the first to admit that not always do I have spiritual thoughts about everyone I meet. My own mind is capable of entertaining some pretty fleshly imaginations. I have recognized this and rely totally on the scriptures of higher thinking in dealing with these scenarios; *II Corinthians 10:5 Casting down imaginations, and every high thing that exalts itself against the knowledge of God, and bringing into captivity every thought to the obedience of Christ.* This means that we can expect to receive imaginations that exalt themselves against the position of God or Light in our lives. They will manifest themselves and we will need to cast them down and bring them into the obedience of Christ. But how many of us really do this? Most of us receive these thoughts and imaginations and because they are socially acceptable, we simply allow the thoughts to settle. We may not dwell on them or we may instinctively know that they are not good, but since so many in the world do it, we consider it natural and acceptable. Again, we may admit that it may not be acceptable for us to do as a believer, but society considers it acceptable and so it settles somewhere on the canvas of our mind. Unfortunately, this is not acceptable warfare. You are involved in an outright battle for the audience of your mind, every day and in every way possible. We cannot adopt a Christ like mindset if we are not proactive and conscious. Without consciously casting down vain imaginations, we are actually playing Russian roulette with our destiny, and time is too short and our enemy too advanced to play that game. We must begin to properly understand how the enemy is attacking us and take the necessary action to combat it.

The bible tells us that we are not ignorant of the devil's devices (*II Corinthians 2:11*). Our adversary is not doing anything cutting edge evil to trick us into making decisions. No, he is not producing anything new. His devices have been the same from the Garden of Eden and they are still working to this day. His device has always been to use our thoughts to cunningly offer an appealing alternative to the truth of circumstance. For many of us renewing the mind is very difficult. We have been operating from our feelings and emotions for so long that they have actually become our god. We are even more comfortable when our feelings and emotions are at ease than we are with the condition of our spirit. However, the Spirit is enmity against the flesh and the flesh is enmity against the Spirit. Once we separate the attributes of those two, we can understand how much our adversary uses the feelings and emotions of this world to control our minds. If we are not adamant in our thought process we will find ourselves chasing mirages. Images that look and feel like truth, but in the end – are death. The adversary of our minds has been around the human psyche for thousands of years. He is the most skillful player in the arena of flesh, emotion and desire. He creates predictable pathways of failure for us that can only be corrected by conscious thought. Every action we take must be proactive and consciously reprogrammed by our spirit. Meaning, we must become conscious of our thoughts and imaginations. If we remain content to react to suggestions and the imaginations presented in our thoughts they will dictate our actions leaving us in very dangerous enemy territory. In this state we will find many failings in our interactions. Fleshly manipulations will rule our thought process and without proactive or conscious thought, we will have nothing to combat them. As we lose understanding of the purpose of the Light of Christ, we will also find that our ministry to the lost will not have a great witness. This is not living in victory, but it can all be changed by addressing the LLT process and how we respond to counterfeit feelings. If you desire change, no longer can you accept the first feelings or thoughts you receive as truth and make decisions to run with what your imagination originally puts before you. According to *II Corinthians 10:5* there are thoughts and imaginations placed in our minds by our adversary; *Casting down imaginations, and every high thing that exalts itself against the knowledge of God, and bringing into captivity every thought to the obedience of Christ.* This tells us that not all thoughts and imaginations come from our spirit. There are some thoughts and imaginations that need to be cast down because they are bait, and provide the stage and platform from which **Satan** presents **his** temptations and **his** ideals. He only wants to see if we will swallow the bait of counterfeit feeling. The enemy knows that if he provides a counterfeit lower level opinion to combat the higher thought processes of truth, he can derail our assignments and make those in need of the Love of Christ unreachable and place our witness in stalemate. So first and foremost, we must be conscious that fleshly thoughts do not originate from us but from our adversary. This sinful nature is the lower level process of thought and is counterfeit. Its only purpose is to provide a conflicting lower level opinion that will combat the truth of Love.

THE COUNTERFEIT PROCESS

Oftentimes attack will come to preempt engaging an assignment. Suppose the Father sends you as a laborer in the path of someone. You may not be fully aware that it is an assignment yet. All you know is that there is something 'different' about someone that you have met. Maybe your spirit is leaping within you, much like John the Baptist did in his mother's womb when Mary walked in the room carrying an unborn Messiah. Or, maybe you get an uneasy feeling around another person. It can range from comforting and pleasurable, to extreme disgust. Now, when we are internally disgusted, it may stem from the fact that either someone is cosmetically repulsive (sight, body odor etc.), or they have offended us, or maybe we have simply misjudged them in some way.

Any determinations made because of cosmetic assessments like a bad odor or unfavorable appearance, is a fleshly determination. When flesh sits in the seat of judgment, it will draw conclusions that oppose the true nature of our assignment. Other times, it may be an attraction or an open door the Father has provided to someone that receives you well that spark counterfeit feeling. Maybe you are being embraced or recognized for your good works, your apparel, physical attraction and the like. Essentially the enemy is trying anything to restrain us from connecting on a higher level (of spirit) and operating in conscious pro-action. This is where ministry actually begins, and religious traditions of men must find its end.

The tradition of most four-wall organizations say, "Flee! Flee! Run, the other direction! This is an 'appearance of evil'. This is jeopardizing the anointing, ruining your witness and looks just WRONG..." If the lower level thought (LLT) process has not been reprogrammed, most good followers of the faith will end any further communique and engagement here. Either they 'do not want to stumble' or assume that the sin of the other person and their fleshly desire will never allow them to hear the gospel we speak. I have heard many opinions on this course of reactions, but hear me when I say this, *"Unless the Holy Spirit has spoken to you and said, '**FLEE**!' this action and subsequent feelings stem from blatant **self-righteousness** and divine mis-judgment."*

After having successfully *avoided* the 'temptation' we then consider it a win over that *test* of flesh and we are proud of our overcoming of the situation. "Yay!" we internally exclaim. Surely we have showed the Devil who is boss, and heaven is undoubtedly applauding our self-control. And so we notch off another "close call but victorious" mark on our self-righteousness belt and feel that we are maturing. Somehow, we *never* take into consideration that the enemy purposely sends "counterfeit" feelings of lower level thoughts. They take the form of fleshly desires and the fault finding misjudgments that *block* what the Spirit of God is saying about a person, a situation or opportunity. Oftentimes, there was never any real threat to our Light, but because of our acceptance of the secular norm, we are actually running away from assignments of ministry. This mentality, has to change. To be honest, *instead of actually overcoming sin, we are simply running from light weight demonic darts* that are battles the Father intends for promotion. Do not get me wrong here, running is definitely sometimes in order. Joseph definitely needed to 'run' from Potiphar's wife as she tried to physically force him into sin. In these instances, boldly follow the voice of the Holy Spirit within and flee! But let's not equate an all-out physical attack on your character with a simple dart of lower level thinking.

Instead of overcoming sin, we are simply running from light weight demonic darts.

We should not be ignorant of our enemy's ploy to use counterfeit thoughts and feelings to encourage us to react and keep us from operating in the purity of truth and greater purpose of our assignment. Instead of reacting to these initial suggestions of the flesh, we should consciously look behind the counterfeit and see the intended purpose. Personally, I find that sometimes the enemy unwarily helps me fulfill assignments that I would have otherwise missed because his fight for me to adopt these counterfeit feelings is so strong.

A practical example of Satan helping us fulfill our assignments:
My wife and I often share meals and family game time with other couples and families. One time in particular I can recall I was faced with some of these lower level counterfeit feelings. After our day of fellowship and jovial interactions together with a few families, we all returned to our respective homes but I was left thinking about one lady. Now, she was an

attractive woman so immediately the darts of lower level thinking were saying, "Lust. Lust. This is Lust, you must avoid future interaction with her." But instead of ending here, I cast down the wicked and counterfeit imaginations about this lady and reprogrammed my thought patterns about her. So instead of allowing my mind to ramble with secular thoughts, my thoughts became, 'What do I have to offer as a brother, to my sister in Christ, that will help fulfill her destiny or greater purpose?' *This completely shifted the kind of thoughts that were now allowed an audience in my mind. Once I was opened up to receive my higher assignment and hear what the Spirit of God would say, The Father would speak to me concerning her life and how I should pray. I began to hear and see differently. I would recall certain things she said during our families' time together. These things would stand out and replay over in my spirit. Essentially, these replayed snippets of conversation became prayer points. I was actually being downloaded prayer points and being shown open doors that I could now intercede on for my sister! These things would have never happened without me consciously making a decision to think like Christ and change my lower level process of thought.*

Honestly, to this day I still battle with rejecting the lower level processes of thought and recognizing counterfeit feelings as such. This will never change. As long as we have an enemy, he will stay faithful to his job and throw wicked darts to knock us off course. Like Paul says, I die daily.

This is a daily character development that is not an easy road. We are training ourselves to navigate a narrow path and difficult way. It is definitely not the wide and comfortable path of destruction. It would have been easy for me to take the self 'righteousness' route and superimpose a spot light of mis-judgment on my sister as something else other than what the Father intended. I could have easily allowed that extra attention or 'attraction' to be identified as lust (counterfeit), or maybe I could have identified it as manipulation on her part and aborted the assignment before it began all because I wanted to feel like **I was** *righteous*.

A few years prior, I probably would have simply cut communication and she would not have known why I was ignoring her and her family, nor would she have any idea that I had judged her and our interaction as such. I would have never reached out to her by email and never inquired of her life and hobbies or accepted an invitation to go running. I would have missed out on what turned out to be a very important assignment, of which has blessed both our families' lives over the years. All in efforts to maintain my righteousness, which the Bible tells us is compared to filthy rags anyway.

The desire to pro-act in all that we do must take preeminence. We must renew our mind as it pertains to dealing with the lower processes of thought and counterfeit feeling of the enemy by casting down wicked and vain imaginations about our brothers and sisters. We can then corporately move past the counterfeit feelings of the enemy trying to keep us from sharing Christ with others. Let us not allow *pride* to keep us from establishing these much needed and meaningful relationships.   If we continue to think more highly of our external beauty than our internal, we will always think people are attracted to us when in actuality- *our spirit is the greatest attractor.* Our spirit is Light and it will attract those in the darkness seeking Light.   We need to understand this and prepare ourselves to act like we are the carriers of Light and stand ready to minister to those in darkness. Our spirit is by far the greatest attraction we will ever possess. We are a city set on a hill. The Light of the world.

If we say we contain the spirit of Christ but our flesh is the most attractive attribute about our person, we may need to reevaluate our eternal condition.

The particular lady in this chapter later wrote me a Father's Day email that totally blessed me. I never knew that the very thing I debated demonstrating, helped to free her from a life long struggle.

Here are a few of those words:

"*I've been trying to find the words to explain to you how grateful I am that God brought you into my life - for a variety of reasons. One of those reasons was so that He could re-instill my hope/belief that there are men out there who are GOOD. I know all are human, and fall short, but I was really starting to wonder where all the godly, compassionate, caring and overall decent men went! Thanks for being you, thanks for serving an audience of one, thanks for loving Jen*(my wife)*, and thanks for breaking the mold. I am frustrated as I type this knowing these words are not conveying the heart of the message I am trying to send. I guess unless you have experienced my past files you could not grasp the depth of the refreshment your character and integrity have been in my life. I'll just pray God connects our spirits and does the translating for me. :-) HAPPY FATHER'S DAY!!!*"

Love, Your Sis

6

Operating in the Higher Thought Life!

It should not be a surprise that most people, both the churched and unchurched, are totally opposed to accepting a conscious school of thought. This school of thought takes much effort and quite frankly does not mix well with popular trends. Every day we experience low level thoughts and imaginations that are triggered by our surroundings. Mainstream networks of today broadcast such sexually explicit visuals that even the most rambunctious purveyor of Sodom and Gomorrah would have to raise a brow. This causes the human mind to have a hard time believing the truth about positive intimacy and how we are created for connection.

When the Light of truth becomes so demonized that fleshly desire is now applauded, the lines between what we should and should not do can become quite difficult to decipher. It is often asked, *"How is it possible to operate like this?"* and *"Is this really sustainable?"*

Not only is this type of thought life possible and sustainable, but with our self-indulgent culture of today largely drowning out the voice of the giver of Light, it is absolutely necessary. Everywhere you turn someone is talking about their personal comforts and campaigning for another form of human right. Society has become so fixed on loving self and unashamedly desiring pleasure, that self-comfort has been highly positioned above all else. This makes operating in unconditional Love very difficult since it is neither instinctive, reactive nor a product of our fallen nature.

To operate in Agape Love is a disciplined behavior and we must be conscious enough to recognize that we need to reprogram our mind. This process is not easy. We have learned certain behaviors from many years of experiencing TV, radio, movies and community preaching the same message of self-service. It is automatic for our natural-born sin nature to be subject to the desires of our flesh but there is nothing about thinking consciously that is automatic.

Another one of my mentors, Dr. Patricia Bailey, puts it this way, "God created the world the way He wanted it, now He wants it the way He created it." We were not created to be self-serving and full of selfish ambition. That sin nature happened as a result of being separated from our Creator, the source of Life. When Adam sinned the judgment of God was that he would die and be internally disconnected from God. We are now reconnected to the source of life by the sacrifice

Jesus made on Calvary. We must not devalue the sacrifice He made and live like children of darkness. The prevalence of sin and darkness in the world does not determine whether or not we put Christ first in our interactions with the lost.

Maybe the world does not understand your actions or state of mind. I understand. Quite frankly in so choosing this type of unpopular conscious thought, many of us carry feelings of un-holiness and un-righteousness. You may ask, *"How can someone Love like Christ or think like this with a mind like I have?"*

Again, I understand this thought process, but what we are striving for is **not** the wide road. This is the narrow path, and the difficult way. Our feelings of inadequacy to walk this path of higher thinking is very understandable, and there is actually support for this reality in scripture. In Deuteronomy 9:5, God is speaking through Moses to the children of Israel who thought the very same way. He said, **"It is not because of your righteousness or the uprightness of your heart that you go in to possess their land, but because of the wickedness of these nations that the Lord your God drives them out from before you, and that He may fulfill the word which the Lord swore to your fathers, to Abraham, Isaac, and Jacob."** God was warning the children of Israel to not think they were adequate enough to perform any portion of the responsibilities He set for them to accomplish. In fact, He wanted them to know that the only reason He was giving them these responsibilities, was because the dark wickedness of the world was so great. God was not trusting them because of their adequacy or righteousness. No. In fact, He was only calling them to this assignment because the world was dark. The darkness of the world was so great, He simply needed a willing vessel that He could put His Light in.

You see, God does not hide us or force us away in reaction to the darkness of the world; He *does not* react. He actually calls us to action during the darkest of times. It does not matter how clean or righteous we are, He only needs a willing vessel to shine His Light through. He pro-acts from His nature, and His plan, and this is what makes Him God. The world will always be dark and wicked in nature, just like God will always be Light and the great physician. For this reason, He promotes us, puts His Light in us and commands us to adamantly shine during the darkest of times and to the darkest of people. It is at these times of utter darkness that the world needs to hear, needs to see and needs to encounter the Light and higher level thinking more than ever.

However not everyone is immediately excited to see Light shining when they are in darkness. I am certain there were times you have been asleep and someone enters your room and turns on the light. You are pretty perturbed at the fact that their actions caused you to wake up from a comfortable sleep. You experienced an awakening from a sleep that may have lasted minutes or hours, but imagine the shift in those that have been asleep in their reactive thinking for years, or decades. Some react in joy, understanding that they are finally conscious after being asleep for so many years. For them it is a joy to bring an answer to endless cycles of reaction based nightmares, but for others, it may not be an easy transition. They will voice their disapproval to you in many forms, but remain encouraged. Just keep believing. Keep supporting them and encouraging them to press towards the mark of the higher calling. You are aiming to become a master at allowing Light to shine through you. Let nothing dissuade you. Keep pressing towards the mark of the mind of Christ and you will see things beyond your ability.

RECEIVE, BELIEVE and ACT

What does it take to operate in the higher thought life? This make or break question is really answered in our ability to understand. Once we receive the understanding of **who** we are (*Light of the world*), believe **what** we have (*the mind of Christ*) and **act** on it regardless of what darkness or the fallen nature may dictate, we are operating in the mind of Christ. It does not require the laying on of hands, 40 days of fasting and prayer or any other ceremonial outer workings of man. It is an understanding we receive, believe and practice daily.

Think about how our lower thought life was established. We experience situations and circumstances of the world and they program our predictable responses. By simply watching TV shows, listening to music and watching video streams on the internet, we have defined what the world around us is like. Through value paradigms established through social acceptance, we each have predetermined who we can approach for business, ministry or conversation and how they may respond. Unconsciously, we accept past-files about people groups and other ethnicities even though we may never have met them. We structure our understanding of what our world will be like before we even experience it, and most of this occurs by what we experience through the window of media.

We only have to live and breathe and we will experience situations that create the belief system that we now act on. Just as a reaction based lifestyle is received, believed and manifested in our daily actions, we can also embrace a proactive lifestyle that is received, believed and then acted upon.

Again, we are not trying to attain something that we do not already have. The Light is already in you. You simply need to learn how to get from behind the comforts of the secular nature that hides its brightness. We have to decide to let our Light shine. We do not have to force it or try to work extra hard to make it shine, we just let it shine by not hiding.

Here is a practical example of how being conscious to not abide by the comforts of the masses can allow His Light to shine through us in unchartered territory:

<u>A Shining Light made possible through Higher Thought:</u>
I often travel internationally and this has allowed me to meet many different people from various backgrounds. On this particular trip I was in Muar, Malaysia attending an international school that lasted approximately 18days. This 2½ week intensive included classes from early morning to late night. There were men and women from every walk of life, from clergy to business people and government officials. We all lived in close quarters since this city was in a rural area quite a distance from Kuala Lumpur and there were no major hotel chains there. We ate together in the morning and in the evenings and had a few moments of fellowship around those times. During these times there was a particular elder woman that caught my attention. She had mangy hair and did not wear the nicest clothes and gave off a sense of introversion or seclusion that caused many people to not spend too much time

talking to her. Yes, this was a spiritual school with mature believers in attendance, but you can only press so much before dialogue turns into an unwelcoming one way street. Even in this early point in my life with Christ I was beginning to understand counterfeit feelings and operating in higher thought a little more. So though there was no sense of attraction, I immediately picked up on the sense of distraction. I kept it in mind and sought the Father about what to say to this woman. Though I asked He never spoke a word concerning her. One Sunday morning during praise and worship service, I found myself standing next to her. I did not think much of it immediately, but just began to worship. All of a sudden this burden of Love entered my heart for her that I did not know what to do with. Again, she was not easy on the eyes and her distant personality made it even harder to connect but I just felt like I wanted to embrace her. During worship service I would look over at her a few times out of one eye to see if there was an open door for a hug, but she was so intent on focusing on the Lord it felt sacrilegious to interrupt, even for a hug. So I just gently placed my hand on her shoulder and left it there as we finished praise and worship. The service started and we never spoke a word. It was admittedly quite confusing to me especially with the darts from the enemy, "Oh, so you are trying to prey on older people now? You are disgusting!" I just casted the thoughts down and went about the day. Later that night I saw this lady after dinner. She approached me and said, "So how long have you been a *healing evangelist?" At first, I looked around to see whom she was talking to because she spoke with such confidence, like this was a continuing conversation. "Excuse me?" I said. "Yes, how long have you been in the healing ministry?" she responded. By this time I laughed a little and said, "Can't say I am any healing minister but whatever the Father says, I will do." She then went on to explain that she had been dealing with excruciating pain for 10+ years. The pain never stopped and was getting progressively worse over the years and nothing she had done helped bring her body back into balance. She went on to say that the moment I placed my hand on her shoulder, the pain that had been there for years immediately went away. She could not believe it. She thought it was temporary and so she didn't say much during the service. Yet, it had not come back for the entire day and she was overjoyed. Her countenance changed and she became more interactive and conversing. The Father had done a major work through a mindset that chose to operate in a higher thought life and allow His Light to shine.*

As I share this story, I feel so blessed to have the mind of Christ. This higher thought life is so liberating to you and those around you, that it makes you dangerous so the enemy will do everything he can to crush you and discourage you from operating in higher thought but you must press. The thoughts he put in my mind about preying on older people and the source of my Love were really believable at the time. This woman was the polar opposite of me and to me there was nothing attractive about her flesh, but the adversary is such a deceiver that he had me believing the Agape Love that filled my heart was fleshly... and I almost believed him!

Again, this is not a wide or easy road we are talking about, but a narrow path of conscious thought that will be furiously challenged by our enemy. We must learn to LET the Light of Christ shine by operating in higher thought no matter how the enemy challenges us. I did not have to MAKE my Light shine. I did not have to consciously lay hands on the woman for her to receive her healing. Actually, I did not even know there was (dis)ease in her shoulder. I simply allowed the Light of Christ to shine through me, in Love, and the Light found the dark hidden places of pain that needed to be exposed and surrendered to the cross. *This is in you already.* We just learn to get out of lower level thinking (flesh) and act.

I often think, "What if she never came back and told me she was healed?" I would only have the darts of the enemy and no proof that what I did was of the Lord. Believe me, not everyone will come and thank you, or write you a note, or even say good things about you. Just be encouraged that you are being obedient to what you are *(Spirit – not flesh)*, what is in you *(Light/Mind of Christ)* and what you are commissioned to do *(Let the Light shine).* Even if you 'FEEL' un-anointed or you feel like there is no physical or actual difference between you and the world. Keep pressing towards the mark of Christ.

BUT I AM NO DIFFERENT!

Admittedly, the world around us is very enticing. It is geared to appeal to the flesh and oftentimes we feel drawn to do the exact same things the masses do. Honestly, some of us may ask, "How do I begin to engage this thought life that is so different, when I sometimes desire to be just like everyone else?" At some point in our walk in Christ we have felt the burden of carrying the Light of Christ in a dark world. There are times that we may shun conscious thought simply because we want to be comfortable, and do what everyone else is doing. But remember, carrying the cross of salvation is not a relaxed post. It takes effort to be conscious. It calls you to stand apart from the masses and oftentimes our LLT process is telling us to blend in and be just like everyone else. So this can make it difficult to envision making a conscious change when our thoughts are sometimes following the same path of wickedness, destruction and self-service.

Yes, we all feel ourselves wanting to be served. We all desire intimacy. Most of us strongly desire physical connection and contact. We desire to be told we are pretty and attractive. These are natural feelings that we cannot deny exist, so when we look at the outside world and desire the feelings and fulfillment of it, we can find ourselves questioning the reality of what is really different between us and secular nature.

"Am I really different from the world, if my thoughts seem to align with theirs?"
"Does Light really dwell in me if I desire so much of the world around me?"

These lower level thoughts plague us all. When they are not properly captured, they result in us disqualifying ourselves from acting on what we truly have within. We have probably read the following scripture many times, **Ephesians 2:8 'It is by grace we are saved through faith and not of ourselves; it is the gift of God.'** This scripture explains that nothing about our Light is of ourselves. It is a gift of God. We nullify the value of God's gift in us when we lean on the arm of the flesh. We cannot afford to measure our ability to do anything in our assignment based on our own works. If we desire to Love as Christ, we need to receive and believe as Christ. To the degree that we desire to have a higher thought life, we need to accept that a higher thought life is now our reality.

After we accept that a higher thought life is possible, we then begin to protect it. To Love as Christ, we have to protect these mental processes and practice consciously choosing a higher level of thought. There is a reason not many people operate in Agape Love towards one another. It is far too easy to be about self and the convenience of my schedule and the needs of my family. Everything in life speaks to comfort (of self) and convenience (of self) and making one's *self* better. Everything around us is self-centered. From marketing to music, we find that self-pleasure, sexuality, ambition and the comfort of convenience sells. So without wanting or even desiring otherwise, we are already being taught subconscious programs of lower level thinking (LLT). Once inside us, lower level thinking (LLT) will continue screaming for a prominent place amongst our actions that is all about self. It will scream, **"Make Me Happy!" "I Want to Feel Needed!" "What about Me**?!"

If you were to take an objective look at your everyday life experience, it would baffle you to see the many times we are compelled to protect ourselves and promote our causes, even at the expense of another. It is engrained in our culture, applauded in our business success and rewarded through marketing. Although we know that the Bible says we should '*Esteem others higher than yourselves (**Phil 2:3**)*', and '*Do not just look out for your own interest, but also look out for the interests of others (**Phil 2:4**)*', and '*To save your life you must lose it, but if you lose your life you will save it (**Matt 6:25**)*'. These are all biblical truths in scripture that we may have quoted at some point in our lives, but living out these scriptures requires a thought life that is not automatic.

The higher thought life embodies the truth of scripture. It is adamant, conscious and completely against the cultural norm. Our society is now competing with more violent displays of selfish ambition than ever before and it is starting younger every year. Unfortunately we are experiencing an increase in these selfish ambitions and fleshly freedoms at the same time that we have handcuffed parental competence.

The parental correction methods that once raised our adolescents are now abusive and socially taboo and so have been replaced with encouraging our children to become more self-aware through encouraging curiosity and 'exposure' to outside elements even if they are dark.   In a controlled environment this type of curious learning and exposure can be beneficial to the development of a growing mind. However, when the exposure is in a culture steeped in selfish ambition, convenience and modern infatuation with idle chatter via social media outlets that lack anything of substance, we breed a petri dish of emotional instability and flesh driven curiosity. Remember flesh is never satisfied and knows no bounds. We must grasp the understanding of a higher thought life so that we can be aware of these traps and train our generation on how to avoid them. We cannot afford to allow the LLT process an audience with our younger generation when technology is providing such an ease of access to an abundance of self-pleasing activities, pornography, prostitution, dirty dancing, stripping, violence, drugs and the glorification of substance abuse. These experiences hinder Agape from developing in relationships and actually supercharges the lower level nature that destroys our ability to place any value in a higher thought life.

Make the decision to operate in a higher thought life today. This is a thought life that is not reactionary and predictable, but a process that causes you to be conscious of all the vain imaginations and thoughts that come to your mind. We should be casting down imaginations every day, every hour and every minute. As long as we are thinking we are commanded to capture our thoughts and line them up with Christ. Do not allow any thought or imagination to settle in your mind without purpose. Even if you do not intend to act on it, do not let it remain. Cast it down in the name of Jesus and replace it with conscious thoughts of Life. Beloved, choose Life and create the destiny you were chosen to fulfill by consciously framing your thoughts, every second of every day.

7

a Talk with **TED**...

If there were any classification of people that we could unanimously agree have a skewed viewpoint of relationships, I think it's those who have been accused of rape or serial murder. Surely rapists and serial killers do not understand the message of *'esteem others higher than yourself'* and Agape Love is probably not their strongest character attribute. The life choices convicted of these crimes has largely condemned them to an anti-culture of our society. However, if we choose not to simply avoid them but to educate ourselves on the conditions that created and fed the wickedness of their mentalities, we will understand the weapons and nature of our adversary.

We can find interviews with some of these people and gain insight to the internal workings of their lower level thought (LLT) process. They have been studied and interviewed by numerous professionals, psychoanalysts and Christian leaders. These transcripts can help us understand what common factors were present that could have encouraged and made way for such darkness. We can learn what fed and watered their thought process throughout the years and gain understanding on the type of experiences at home, at school and in what they considered entertainment that furthermore fed their decisions making. Once we allow these events to surpass subconscious entertainment and transpose them to conscious learning, we create a powerfully comprehensive dialogue that will help future generations avoid the same pitfalls.

Dr. James Dobson is recorded in a powerful and telling interview with convicted rapist and serial killer Ted Bundy. The day before Ted Bundy was to be executed he made conscious statements about what he felt gave birth to the compelling evil inside him. Throughout the interview Ted demonstrates a remorseful sober mind. Now separated from the environment that once fed his desire, he was contrite and conscious. For the evils he committed against society, he now faced the death penalty and though he desired to live, he knew society felt it had to rid the world of people like him. What I witnessed in the transcripts of this interview was a broken and now blatantly honest man describing the source of the dark energy that worked through him and others he met while in prison. He was able to identify the evil that gripped him deep inside his Christian led home, and expose it. He felt that if society did not deal with the darkness it would produce the same energy that operated in him and cause more people to go down the same path he did.

As you read the following transcript try to recognize the LLT process that grew in him, even while in the environment of a Christian led home. Be conscious as you read that you are not just reading for entertainment, but you are reading this to train your consciousness and to learn the devices of our adversary.

When asked about his childhood and what, if anything, led to him committing such heinous acts, Ted Bundy responded:

"I wasn't a pervert in the sense that people look at somebody and say, 'I know there's something wrong with him.' I was a normal person. I had good friends. I led a normal life, except for this one, small but very potent and destructive segment that I kept very secret and close to myself." He goes on to say, *"Those of us who have been so influenced by violence in the media, particularly pornographic violence, are not some kind of inherent monsters. **We are your sons and husbands. We grew up in regular families.** Pornography can reach in and snatch a kid out of any house today. It snatched me out of my home 20 or 30 years ago. As diligent as my parents were, and they were diligent in protecting their children, and as good a Christian home as we had, there is no protections against the*

kinds of influences that are **loose in a society** that tolerates (this)..."

Essentially he was pleading with the masses to wake up and do something with the sexualization of our culture via pornography. He was trying to point us to the understanding that no matter how meaningless or harmless viewing violent pornography may seem, it should _not_ be considered a healthy form of entertainment. By all his accounts, it was severely damaging to any mind that it inhabited. Dr. James Dobson continues on and asks him about his findings while living amongst the inmates in prison over the years.

Dobson asks, "...*You feel that hardcore pornography, and the door to it, softcore pornography, is doing untold damage to other people and causing others to be abused and kill the way you did?*"

Bundy responds, "*I'm no social scientist, and I don't pretend to believe what John Q Citizen thinks about this, but I've lived in prison for a long time now, and I've met a lot of men who were motivated to commit violence.* **Without exception, _every one of them was deeply involved in pornography_ – deeply consumed by the addiction.** *The F.B.I.'s own study on serial homicide shows that the most common interest among serial killers is pornography.*"

When asked whether people should forgive him he stated, *"I hope that those who I have caused so much grief, even if they don't believe my expression of sorrow, will believe what I'm saying **now**; there are those loose in their towns and communities, like me, **whose dangerous impulses are being fueled, day in and day out, by violence in the media** in its various forms – particularly sexualized violence. What scares me is when I see what's on cable T.V. **Some of the violence in the movies that come into homes today is stuff they wouldn't show in X-rated adult theatres 30 years ago.**"*

And all this is being said in the mid 90's. Frankly, I find this astonishing when you look at where the movie industry and mainstream TV networks have pushed the envelope in the areas of soft porn and slasher type violence in the 21st century. It is no wonder why we continue to struggle to heal and engage in positive intimacy with clear intention.

When Ted Bundy was asked whether he felt he deserved the punishment the state had relegated him, he said, *"...I'm talking about going beyond retribution, which is what people want with me. There is no way in the world that killing me is going to restore those beautiful children to their parents and correct and soothe the pain. But there are lots of other kids playing in streets around the country today who are going to be dead tomorrow, and the next day,* **because other young people are reading and seeing the kinds of things that are available in the media today.***"*

Ted Bundy not only admits that pornographically violent media broke through the protections of his religious childhood and opened the door to the heinous acts he committed, but he also said that without exception, everyone else in the prison also had the exact same habit. We can take this as coincidence and label them as abnormal outside characters totally foreign to our processes of thought, or we can learn about how the devices of devil worked here.   "***Lest Satan should get an advantage of us: for we are not ignorant of his devices.***" 2 Corinthians 2:11. Since we are not ignorant of the way the adversary works, our eyes are open to his plan to keep us bound to reactionary low level thinking.

This was such an eye opening statement that when I personally read this interview for the first time, I literally left it up on my computer screen for days. I would often re-read it and shake my head in disbelief that he was so blatant and direct about what opened the door of evil delusion and spurned the downward spiral of reaction that led to the demise of numerous women. I mean, the darkness of his heinous acts were so gruesome that he became famous. Unfortunately, instead of learning from him and what might have caused this evil, we made movies, demanded 'justice' and we were very curious to learn about the gory details of his story. We simply focused on the LLT portion of appeal.

One would think that hearing this man explain what fed and inspired him to such great evils would be a huge awakening for our society. Our conscious minds should have been pricked to their core. The understanding that another device of our adversary had been exposed should have at least caused us to pause, take note and create public outcry as a corporate body to prevent more of the same from happening again in our society. But instead of awakening and operating from that higher plane of thought, we remained asleep.

Since the mid 90's, we actually have become more 'accepting' of violence and over sexualization in our culture. The same material that inspired Ted Bundy and many others to travel down a destructive path that affects us all is still being sold and consumed in mass quantities. Not only did we remain asleep, but our culture also began to accept over-sexualization as a means for profit and started promoting new levels of violence and sexuality in movies, in cartoons and even video games! And if that were not enough, at the same time, our culture became more outwardly brazen in demonizing the voices that support traditional intimacy, relational responsibility and monogamy. Many now believe that the views of traditional intimacy and monogamy are antiquated and cannot apply to such an advanced modern culture.

From all points of view the floodgate of erotic sexual acceptance is widening. It is becoming increasingly powerful for use in marketing. We have recognized its destructive power but have also chosen to use its influence to prey on those who are unconscious while we line our pockets with gain. Corporately, we cannot expect social normalcy to embrace conscious thinking. All indications in scripture say that as time progresses, society will become more perilous and more reactionary to the desires of the flesh. We must gain understanding of what is Light and what is of the Darkness and beware of *those who call Good evil and evil good, who put darkness for light and light for darkness."* Isaiah 5:20

We have read scripture. We know truth and see it, but what are we going to do about it? If we do not make the choice to consciously reprogram our actions and understand our Light, we will fall victim to the lower level thought processes of reaction and fleshly desire, which scripture tells us results in death. There is a reason our relationships with the opposite gender always tend to end up fleshly. It should not be, but it has been planned that way. There is a reason why the thought of esteeming others higher than ourselves is backwards. It should not be and it does not have to continue. There is a reason we are not experiencing the effective Love of Christ in our witness, and it all stems from us not recognizing the devices of our enemy and making the choices to operate in a higher thought life.   There are many news reports and other interviews just like this one between Dr. James Dobson and Ted Bundy that can teach us many secrets about how our enemy operates.   Let us not be ignorant of the devices of our enemy.   Scripture says that "**wisdom cries aloud in the streets**" Proverbs 1:20.   We must develop the ear to hear.   The signs are all around us.   Beloved, let us be conscious of the wisdom that cries out in our everyday lives, and let us learn from others.

8

The Stimulus Response

One day, press 'pause' and take an objective look at the surface level of human interaction around you. I invite you to become an eye-witness of how anemic the depth of positive intimacy really is. Consider the evidence; no eye contact, limited conversation, and distracted dialogue – the kind of communication that occurs when people are multi-tasking while they talk to you. For example, the bus ride, where no one looks up from their personal devices the entire time. The airplane ride, where many are cold yet cordial, and unnatural responses are the expected norm. Think of your neighbor whom quickly closes the garage to avoid interaction. Maybe that is you. Think about the family who sends texts from upstairs to ask if dinner is ready. Maybe this is your family. Consider our modern day customer service worker, who fails to greet customers entering their store. What about the distant 'church hug' that leaves you feeling more isolated than embraced? We could continue for days. Fact is, our modern social culture lacks connection and is in dire need of adjustment.

Most of us admittedly are keenly aware of the mass introversion and failings of our communities, yet we have not taken action to demand change in our own lives. However, we were created to be different, and we can be different.

This conscious place of higher level thought transcends simply helping to increase interaction and connectivity between opposing genders. This conscious thought can also be used to short circuit ANY reactionary stimulus response. When the understanding of what is in you (Light) and it purpose (shine in dark places) is placed into action by a conscious mind, it will change reactionary responses to race relations, systemic injustice and internal self-confidence and self-esteem issues.

What we hear, what we see and what we experience all play a vital role in creating a belief system of character and faith that confirm our actions. As the bible says, *"Faith comes by hearing..."* Romans 10:17, our belief system to react or pro-act is a choice based on what we give our attention to. If we never choose to reprogram our minds, we are making a decision to be engineered by what we see or hear or experience around us every day. No matter if we agree with the sexualization of marketing advertisements, cinema entertainment or the experiences and choices of our peers. If we are not consciously choosing our thought projections and paths, by default we are accepting the path of social acceptance. No matter how fleshly or anti-Christ we may have judged them to be. Simply stated, we make choices based on what we see, experience and hear. This is a spiritual law and marketing companies use this understanding to experience multibillion dollar profits year after year. They know that all they must do is place their product in front the masses and simply insinuate that is good, and they have created a belief system.

Noam Chomsky, modern linguist, philosopher and cognitive scientist co-authored a book called 'Manufacturing Consent", in which it is explained in great detail, the very nature of news outlets and they how corporately use their media platform to manufacture, or create, a consensus amongst the masses.

So ask yourself. Are you a victim of the intelligent minds of our marketing industry and media outlets?   Are you completely subjected to the whims of our surrounding circumstance? You may defiantly shout, "Of course not! No way, not me!" But unfortunately the answer is, yes you are. We all are. You may need to swallow your pride on this one, because unless you are consciously reprogramming your mind on a daily basis, you will not escape what is seen, heard and culturally experienced every day. It is a spiritual law that we will always have faith to do what we give our attentions to. There is no other way around this stimulated response. The only way we can become something other than the product of our environment is to adopt a higher thought life and consciously short circuit our inbred cultural responses.

A stimulus and response example:

You are watching a commercial one evening featuring a cute actress/actor marketing the latest product. At some point in the commercial the model sensually looks into the camera or poses purposely to evoke a sense of desire or passion from you, the viewer. Marketing cultures use these sensual appeals to cause reactionary desire within us, hoping the desires will be projected on to the product. However, in the moment, the medium of stimulus, or what sparks this desire is not the product itself, but the actress or actor. The hope is that in that moment of your desire, they will arouse or create a favorable reaction – need, want or desirable pleasure. If the beautiful actress/actor creates a level of desire in you that now surpasses the desire you have for the advertised product alone, you have experienced stimulus and they are banking on a targeted response. This manufactured response of your desire or want was created by using a sexually desirable model as stimuli. When companies use this stimulus response psychology we become stimulated responders without full understanding of why or how we reached the end result.

The stimulus response is a very powerful mental process that constructs the framework of our mass media. Blame it on capitalism, greed or misdirection of marketing psychology. We can try and blame whomever we will, but in the end the choice to reprogram our thought life is still left with us.

When we choose to reprogram our thought process, we will actually create a file that will forever be stored in the file cabinet of our brain. Once we have a new file history, which we will call a 'past-file', our brain has the ability to use this new experience as a future reality. If we do this often enough it will create a habit that will reset our subconscious responses and eventually totally wipe away the conditioned reactions learned over the years.

The marketing companies have already acquired their target. They unashamedly go after the lower level thought response of our minds. They simply play on the stimulus response of sexual appeal in hopes that it will carry over to their product through our LLT process. Many marketing companies know this appeal is so powerful and effective that they will employ sex appeal without even having a connection to the products being sold. For example, there is a popular internet domain and hosting services company that often uses very racy television ads featuring scantily clad women to advertise their low cost hosting services. A lot of their customer base host sites that operate daycare services, afterschool tutoring programs, repair shops and religious organizations, all of which have nothing to do with sexual appeal. There is absolutely nothing that this racy advertising has in common with this content. However, since promoting sexuality garners attention, attention can breed a need for their product, and when people want their product there are new sales. Motivated by profit, they too are catering to the innate LLT process.

The end goal is to generate dollars. Although the road to profit generation may travel a winding path of sexual imagery ranging from over the top overt, to very subtle, if profits are realized most any company is happy to take advantage of the stimuli response that plays so well with the LLT process of sexualization.

As you make your commitment to reprogram your thought life, you will need to be conscious to take proactive steps to protect against the thought pattern the ads are trying to get you to follow. Everyday experiences with ads like these provide an opportunity to create new past-files and convictions about certain connections, people and sexuality as it relates to the opposite gender. Once experienced, they are filed away as truth and reality in our minds and they are triggered to support the actions of our future life experiences.

For instance, we all typically think of 'heat' or 'light' when we see an image of the sun. These are past-files from previous experiences that now create a stimulus response. To the mind, fire is 'HOT' and ice is 'COLD'. Why? Because of our PAST experiences with fire, cooking or matches that have caused us to FILE the experience away as truth. This past-file now constructs a portion of what is reality to us. We no longer need to touch the flames of a fire pit to know that it is hot. Likewise, if ice cubes were to accidentally fall as you open your freezer and you reach down to pick them up, you probably would not be surprised that the cubes are cold to the touch. This is due to past-files you have created through previous experiences.

In this same manner, our mind has also categorized certain past-files concerning other intangibles like the opposite sex, what Love is, and how we are expected to interact with one another. And unfortunately, most of our past-files have been created through subconscious experiences, based on a secular LLT process. Even if you are a religious leader in a faith based organization who lives a generally 'safe' life, unless you are consciously and consistently recreating your past-files every day, what you are currently experiencing is a reaction based truth stemming from a LLT process. We do not live in a supernatural bubble where we are protected from the opinions, passions and cultural traditions around us. Instead, we are subjected to secular clouds of thought every day at school, our workplace, the gym and right at home via our media devices and television sets. The average home in the U.S. owns 2.5 television sets, making the ideas and culture of secular social acceptance easily accessible.

It is not difficult to see how fleshly stimuli has worked to shape the mind of the average secular individual. However, what is more concerning is when this process of thought is carried into leadership roles within the four walls of local churches and religious organizations. The church is the very place where the lost should come to experience those who live consciously on a higher thought plane (mind of Christ) and have reprogrammed their fleshly stimulus responses. The lost should be afforded the opportunity to enter into the four walls and see Light in operation; Loving them, blessing them and esteeming them higher than those of the church, regardless of stature, race, creed or sexual gender. Unfortunately, many organizations develop rules of restriction simply because of sexualized past-files of what the other gender is capable of doing or desiring and this allows the same secular nature of sexualization in the world to breed in the church. We are Light, but we must be mindful to not bend too far towards the possibilities of what darkness is capable of, instead of walking in what Light is capable of.

As carriers of the Light of Christ, we have done a poor job in allowing the higher mindset of Christ to rule our thought life. Instead of fighting to support a conscious thought life and encouraging other leaders to follow suit, we define our rules of engagement in the same manner in which the disciples judged the interaction between Jesus and the harlot. I do not believe that the only reason Jesus was able to share covenant meals with harlots, tax collectors and others in darkness was because He was perfect in His flesh. Through demonstration Jesus was actually teaching the disciples that we are the answer to the lost, the Light to those in darkness and a healer to those in dis-ease. When Jesus said, "**What good is a physician to them that are already healed?**" Mark 2:17, the question He was actually posing was, 'Are we not supposed to bring balance to imbalanced mindsets?' In essence, the harlot and the tax collector evidently had dis-ease or dis-order in their thought life. Maybe the harlot was experiencing a life threatening imbalance from being lost in darkness that only the Light of Christ could heal. Jesus was not demonstrating that His perfection alone allowed Him to sit at the table and minister to those in darkness. He was simply modeling the actions of a higher thought life. As carriers and containers of Light we have a responsibility to think differently and shine our Light in the darkest of places and to the darkest of people. Darkness should not cause us to hide, nor should it dictate how or when we allow Light to shine. The Light is meant to be shown, to go before our nature and lead the way. How else can the lost see the path? If we do not demonstrate positive intimacy how will the world know how to intimately connect and walk in Love? They will continue to think the only type of intimacy and depth of connection is self-serving and physical in nature and the office of a medic will soon be obsolete.

Later in the book we will discuss the office of Emergency Medical Staff and Medics. I respect their office a great deal and they are a good example of positive intimacy. Positive intimacy is not carnal or erotic in nature. I understand the term intimacy has a very fleshly connotation, but it should not be considered fleshly to the reprogrammed mind. This is why I like to use the example of an EMT in demonstrating how we should act in times of duress or ministry. Most EMTs have to possess a higher thought life when performing their job efficiently. It is a pretty intimate position of vulnerability when someone is dying or in pain. Can you imagine a male EMT showing up to the scene of an accident where an attractive female passenger has been impaled with an object through the chest and all he can think about is her breasts? I am sure the thought of how attractive the woman is may in fact cross the LLT region of his human mind. It may even brighten his day that he has the opportunity to work on such a fine feminine specimen. However, if an EMT is to operate efficiently at their job and be effective, at some point the **wounds** and **life** of the subject must take preeminence over his own LLT process. He must think higher than a low level stimulus response and administer health via tourniquet, pain meds, stint, fluids, stabilizing techniques etc. His life giving role MUST take PREEMINENCE over the innate LLT process for him to be effective.

Much like this EMT, our role as liberators and carriers of Light must also take preeminence if we are to be effective in our assignments as carriers of His Light. It is impossible to think like the world and be effective at administering health and the Light of Christ at the same time.

We must prepare ourselves to reach those that are lost and wandering in the dark. We cannot be afraid to venture where those in darkness dwell. We must meet them in their point of need and at the place where they need it most. We cannot expect them to come search us out in the synagogues, already repentant or in an already fixed state? Jesus instructed us to go. Go into the highways and byways, to people that are vagabonds and have no home or job and may even rob others for a living. We should expect to be dealing with the broken and dis-eased (those trapped in a lower level thought life) and should prepare ourselves to administer health and balance on a daily basis. Too often, we reject a proactive conscious thought pattern and accept the LLT process.

This I say, therefore, and testify in the Lord, that you should no longer walk as the rest of the Gentiles walk, in the futility of their mind - Ephesians 4:17

We are firmly instructed not to conduct ourselves in the same fashion as the world. More specifically scripture tells us we should not think as others think, in the *futility* of the mind. Meaning in the lowliness of our fleshly thoughts. *Our thoughts should be purpose driven and carry life.* The only purpose of our flesh, is to die. Yes, flesh is a carrier of our spirit and houses life, but flesh is born to die. The average human body has billions of skin cells, and between 30,000 and 40,000 of those fall off every hour of the day. So this means that in a 24-hour period we lose almost one million skin cells. Yes, almost 1 million skin cells of our flesh die every day. Flesh is a very temporary conduit whose end goal is death. This is evident in the dust that collects in our houses, on our tables, TV, windowsills and on those picture frames that are so hard to get clean. All that is made mostly from dead human skin cells. We each give dust mites over 8lbs of food every year from our dead flesh. This is probably uncomfortable to think about but this should help create a visual of how temporary and lowly our flesh is. We are more than dust mite food and we were not created to simply enjoy fleshly desires. Plainly stated, we were born into a sinful nature of futility. It is inbred in our nature to desire comfort, ease and convenience which are all subconscious reactions. However, this futility of lower level thinking is not our created purpose and should never govern our interactions. It is the end result of our minds being disconnected from purpose.

In the beginning Adam and Eve had instructions to not eat of the tree of Knowledge of Good and Evil or they would die. The Creator was telling man that once you decide you know what is right or wrong without me, you will be lost to the lower level thought process forever. Flesh is never satisfied. Once the mind gets a taste of comfort, convenience, control and desire, why would it want to stop experiencing it? Stop for what? The flesh wants more and more of itself until death destroys its ability to contain anything else. Our separation from the Creator in the Garden, separated man from the higher purpose of dominion and subjected us to the futility of our flesh. This is why we need Jesus. We needed someone that could forever short circuit the stimulus response that naturally operates in our mind since this fall in the Garden. The Father is instructing us in Ephesians 4 to put off the condition of futility, uselessness and lower level thinking. He is instructing us to think in a manner that is life giving and purposeful. Those who come around us should feel refreshed and honored to be in our presence. Not because of all the worldly accolades we have amassed, but because we have a higher thought life thereby making us conduits of purpose, life and unconditional Love.

This higher thought plane is only higher because it is conscious and purposeful. You will not reach this understanding through unconscious effort. Much like falling down a hill maybe effortless, but it is certainly scientifically and physiologically impossible to climb to a hill without exerting effort. To go up, we must be conscious that this is what we intend to do. So when dealing with the flesh and interaction with those of the opposite sex, addiction and anything else on the lower level thought plane, there are a few steps that can aide in consciousness.

Step 1

We must learn to pro-act not react to surrounding circumstance.
Learn not to respond to the first stimulus (thoughts, ideas, suggestions, desire) triggers that marketing media, music and TV use to manipulate us so well. Instead, we must be conscious to pro-act based on a conscious desire to be a liberator and carrier of life and Light to those around us. Flesh is a REACTOR and you can predict how it will respond. Spirit, on the other hand, is PROACTIVE. It is always looking to add life and healing regardless of surroundings or opposition. We

must learn to be proactive and NEVER react to any circumstance or situation. *This must be a continual state of conscious thinking.*

Step 2

Esteem others higher than your past.

The past is filled with lower level thoughts created by unhealthy experiences, over sexualized visual media, movies, books, soft porn, and audio media. All these experiences have programmed a learned response. In this step we learn to consciously reject these responses. You will now seek to consciously reject the popular programmed beliefs that all men are innately animalistic in their conquering. You will now reject the popular programmed beliefs that suggest women are meant to be physically/mentally conquered. Now does this mean that we are to become TOTALLY VULNERABLE with every male or female acquaintance? Certainly not. But this does mean that every situation and every circumstance concerning men should now be approached from a higher thought plane. Likewise, in viewing women, we are not removing the fact that they are attractive, but we are REPROGRAMMING OUR RESPONSE to the attraction of beauty. Esteem others higher than your **thoughts**, your **past**, your **negative experiences**, your **selfish ambitions**...and yourself.

Step 3

Greet one another as family.

I am sure many of us have attractive sons or daughters, brothers or sisters, cousins, aunts or uncles that are beautiful. We look at them, see their beauty and smile with thoughts of appreciation and respectful pride that they are related to us. Mass social acceptance has made it taboo for us to think sexually about our family so certain thoughts are often limited and immediately cast down if ever presented. In the same manner, as our brother's keeper, we must reprogram our thought life and structure it to view others as family. See others as your brother or your sister, as if they carried your same last name and you both grew up in the same household. This higher thought plane of looking at others through the eyes of family is not escapism or a good alternative way to see the opposite gender. No, I did not make up this idea, it is actually the word of GOD. *1 Timothy 5:1-2 1Rebuke not an elder, but entreat him as a father; and the younger men as brothers; 2The elder women as mothers; the younger as sisters, with all purity.* In context, this scripture becomes very weighty. And no, I did not add the last encouragement; "with all purity". Our Father was simply giving us instructions in how to operate in the higher thought life - mind of Christ. He knew we would always receive both attractive stimuli and stimuli that causes distraction. He was giving us instructions to overcome the LLT process concerning those we meet.

When we treat those of the opposite gender as family- in all purity, we are seeking their greater good and can now receive instruction on how to bless them, pray for them and interact with them on that plane.

Step 4

Train yourself to reprogram in the moment.

To achieve a higher thought process, we must strive to operate consciously every day. Paul said, *"I affirm, by the boasting in you which I have in Christ Jesus our Lord, I die daily." - 1 Corinthians 15:31*   When we are consciously reprogramming the mind, we need to understand that it is a daily battle. Every day and every hour or every minute we need to be mentally conscious in the now. In the 2-5 seconds that we make decisions on how to respond, our minds need to be conditioned to be conscious of our purpose and the position we have in the life of the person we are speaking to. In the moment we should always be conscious that our purpose is to shine Light and bring life to every situation, and the person we are speaking to should always be looked at as family.

My father-in-law is a professional natural body builder. When I first met my wife Jennifer, he was greatly inspirational in encouraging my studies of natural holistic medicine and competing as a natural body builder. Because of my success and understanding of muscle building, proper meal preparation and weight training, I have the opportunity to work with many people. This work within the field of health and physical fitness allows me to often speak to attractive women. My mind certainly attempts to run the culturally inspired programs of over sexualization. When these times occur, I have learned to use one of the greatest weapons in the Bible that support operating in a higher thought life. Again, II Corinthians 10:5 is a great foundation scripture to adopt when living a higher thought life. It says...***casting down imaginations and every high thing that exalts itself against the knowledge of God, bringing every thought into captivity to the obedience of Christ...II Corinthians 10:5***

This instructs us to cast down fleshly imaginations and lower level thoughts, and anything that promotes itself over Agape Love. Furthermore, it goes on to say that we should also capture our thoughts and bring them into alignment with Truth (Christ). Imagine that! We are instructed to actually control the flow of information allowed an audience in our conscious mind. When we fail to esteem others higher than the belief systems of this world, we condemn our Light to the recesses of our subconscious. The result leaves us experiencing a defeated life and offering nothing to help others escape the bondage of futility and darkness. Instead of us providing a way of escape or bringing the life of the fruits of the Spirit to those in darkness, we actually collaborate in the bondage to futile thought.

Handle it NOW!

Do not be mistaken, you will probably always see the opposite gender as some sort of sexual representative. As a man, I believe women were created to be the more attractive creation. Women are more beautifully vibrant, soft and curvy of the two genders. Having fathered 5 children, sexuality certainly has a place in my thought life, but that does not mean I am <u>bound</u> to operate solely on sexualized stimulus of thought, especially when dealing with family.

The key is not to fool yourself into believing that sexuality and beauty is of the flesh and no one is beautiful except the Lord. That is religious jargon and is not practical to operating in a higher thought life. We will always see beauty and there will always be attractions and turn offs. But what do these circumstances and interactions cause you to do? Are you reacting or pro-acting? Do you turn away from the repulsive and unattractive, or do you offer the life giving Love of Christ? Do you react in holy introversion around the attractive and physically appealing, or do you cast down imaginations and act like you are your brother or sisters' keeper? Personally, if I am not daily and constantly casting down imaginations, it is hard for me to be effective in ministry. Our reprogramming is in the 'now'. It's the decisions we make in the 2 to 5 second windows of whatever it is that has our attention. This includes glances of the magazine ads at the grocery store, commercials and any other sexually appealing cinematic visuals you see every day.

My family will attest that they always hear me mumbling something throughout the day. My normal reprogramming command is, *"I bind that in the name of Jesus"* or *"I curse that in Jesus' name".* If the lower level dart comes back, I say it again until there is silence or the Holy Spirit replaces whatever counterfeit thoughts the enemy was trying to bait me with. Even while viewing commercials it is not uncommon for me to take actions to avoid receiving subconscious programming. It may seem pretty small, but it starts here in the little changes we make in our day-to-day actions that causes a shift to higher thinking. For instance, if a commercial is portraying someone in an overly sexual manner, I will look away. I have learned that curiosity and mystique is a draw that seems very innocent at first glance, but it often leaves behind subconscious past-files of sexualization that will ruin the ability to intimately interact and Love on others in the future. It is our responsibility to guard against the past-files these visuals can create so that we prepared and ready for the mind of Christ to led our interactions with a possible attraction or aesthetically appealing person of the opposite sex. When we program our minds to truth, interactions can now be on the basis of a brother or sister, in all purity. At this point, the thoughts and imaginations will change from what the person can do for you, into, "How can I serve them? What would you have for me to do and speak to them Father?"

This has radically changed my conversations with others and has allowed for ministry to hidden hurts that only the Light of the Father could find. As a result, it is more normal for me to experience deep positive relationships with others, than it is to have a surface interaction. The fulfillment of being able to minister the Light of Christ to the hidden places of those in my sphere of influence is far more than satisfying than anything the lust of temporary fleshly desires can offer. Besides, no matter how sensually pleasing it may be, the end road of flesh is always some form of death and destruction. Death of relationship. Death of Marriage. Business. You name it. It simply does not profit to operate under the dictates of the flesh.

Again, we should reprogram LLT processes in the moment by simply turning our head from day-to-day experiences in advertising (magazines) and imbalanced commercials and visuals that we believe will produce imbalanced desires. This is not always possible to judge this change from the outside looking in, but the environment of our hearts will be shaped and our thoughts brought into captivity when we operate in the now and are conscious of who we are. Believe me, reprogramming your mind for a higher thought life becomes easier with repetition. Repetitious reprogramming will make your thought life more conscious. This forms a habit of operating in the character of higher thinking. Soon reacting to a LLT process will be repulsive to this new nature.

Unfortunately, most of us will find this method of higher level thinking mentally difficult and too hard, and so will refuse the narrow path and difficult way. But Why? Why refuse to adopt this mentality when great success has been attributed to the forefathers of the faith whom have adopted a higher thought life? It may be different but it is exactly the type of thought pattern that defines the men and women of God in the Bible. Walking in this manner caused them to feel so out of place that they confessed they were strangers and pilgrims on the Earth.

These all died in faith, not having received the promises, but having seen them afar off were assured of them, embraced them and confessed that they were strangers and pilgrims on the earth.- Hebrews 11:13

Though we may only see this unique perspective as something separating us or causing us to be categorized as different by the world, we cannot be discouraged.   Begin to refuse to simply sit passively by and just read about the great exploits of the men and women of God.   We are to read them and be encouraged to emulate them.   They are the great cloud of witnesses that speak of what can be done in Him. We need to hear, read and increase our faith so we can then go out into the world and do greater.   Admittedly, this does require a daily and conscious death to our fleshly desire in order to walk by the spirit.   This is something not readily accepted by a world in bondage to the desires and passions of the flesh, but we must demand this higher thought life no matter how much of a stranger it may make us appear.

9

Strangers & Pilgrims

Your decision to walk in the conscious mindset of Christ is not an easy task. You must be prepared to embrace a lifestyle that is totally different from everything you see, hear and sense. Not simply different because you are now making decisions to pray over your food or attend church on a regular basis. No, the bible actually says you are a stranger and pilgrim, and a rather peculiar person. You are a stranger on a pilgrimage through this modern culture and nothing around you defines you.

Imagine that you are on a mission trip to share the gospel to a remote people group in a rural area. As soon as you land, go through foreign customs and step out of the airport, nothing is familiar. The languages and conversations you hear, all strange. The way the locals are dressed - all foreign. You check into the hotel and on the T.V. there is foreign news talking about things that are strange to you. You order food and something you have not tasted before is prepared. You would probably decide to fast. Maybe you decide to not watch the local TV because you cannot relate to its topics or content. The conversations around you would also seem trivial as you would lack the understanding to gain interest.

Just reading this should make you feel out of place. To be honest, I have felt this many times while traveling on the mission field, but this is not simply describing a foreign mission trip to an unknown land. Do you think the men and women of faith in the Bible only considered themselves to be Strangers and Pilgrims when they traveled? No, they considered everyday life in their own home town a pilgrimage. Their spirit or higher mindset was actually going through the pilgrimage of an earthly experience. Though familiar to them, the things of the earth did not define them.

For better understanding, try re-reading the above imagination and envision the mission field as your daily surroundings, and the mind of Christ, as the Stranger. Our lives should feel much like that stranger and pilgrim visiting a foreign land. When we walk around and hear fleshly conversation around us, it should be strange. The way that the masses dress and sexually advertise themselves, should be foreign to you. The content on TV, reality shows and idle video streams should seem trivial since it does not relate to who you are, nor is it the reason you are on the earth. All this makes having the mindset of Christ in a dark world, a target. When your actions are not within a familiar framework of those around you, expect to be persecuted and ostracized. Being of the same heart, mind and commonality are the glue that create culture and bind community, but we must be mindful that commonality with the secular world is often contrary to the higher thought process. It is rare that the masses embrace a posture that involve **daily** sacrifice for the benefit of others. Prepare yourself to embrace difference and understand that no matter how pure the intention of your heart may be, the world just may not understand your position.

<u>For example:</u>

On a camping trip, I once provided a light for a young girl whom was walking directly behind me. We were in a group of about 50 kids, all middle school ages. We had just finished a hike into the woods and were heading back to the campsite in what seemed like pitch black darkness. Not everyone had a flashlight, and I could hear people taking missteps behind me. I knew a young girl was behind me and though I did not know her well, I felt bad that she could potentially hurt herself while walking over the rough trail terrain without a light. So I took my flashlight and held it in back of me so she could see her way. When we crossed over ravines or I would hear her misstep, I politely asked if she was okay. Even as a young tween, my protective nature as a male was kicking in and the more we walked, the less I felt I personally needed all the light. I actually began to feel I could navigate pretty well in the darkness without my light as my eyes began to adjust. Well, eventually we made it back to camp and she thanked me and we all went back to our respective cabins. To my surprise, the very next day I was the talk of the camp. Everyone had assumed I had taken an interest in this girl and I could not figure out why. Three different people approached me asking me when I began to have a 'crush' on this young lady. I was still baffled until I asked, "What would make you say this? I don't even know her?" When they told me because of the way I took care of her and kept asking her if she was alright on the hike the night before, I could only shake my head in disbelief.

I share this childhood story to illustrate one of my first early lessons: *"Others often mistake kindness for selfish interests and it is rare to genuinely look out for the interests of others."*

Loving others should feel more natural than reciprocal. We were created for connection and to Love one another. One of the most crippling deceptions of our enemy has been to get us to believe that Love needs reciprocation. Once we espouse the belief that Love requires reciprocation, not only are we deterred from giving it since we do not want people to get the wrong idea of us, but we also do not know how to properly receive because we can only assume the intentions of the person being kind to us is seeking to get something in return. Yet, Agape Love is neither earned nor is anyone required to pay for its benefits. It is an unconditional action that is full of Life and we all need it. It is extremely rare that anyone who contains a gift this valuable would simply give it away, but that is exactly what we are called to do. Freely give, and freely receive. Most people in the world only go out of their way for someone when they are desirous to receive something in return. We train our kids and pets to obey us not simply because it is right, but for a reward. Our early programming was not based on doing unto others as you would have them do unto you, but rather if you do this it will qualify you to receive this.

Scripture encourages us to think differently than the social norm. The mind of Christ makes it rain on both the just and unjust. God causes circumstances to benefit both those who good and those who are evil. He says, ***Love your enemies and pray for those who use you. Likewise He causes the sun to rise on both those who are good and those whom operate with evil –Matthew 5:45*** Then he defines the higher thought process of Christ in the next verse. ***If you love those who love you, what reward will you get? Are not even the tax collectors doing that? - Matthew 5:46***

Scripture makes it abundantly clear that we should do good to others whether we like them or not. Friend or foe, we should Love them and demonstrate good works and go out of our way for them. This is the mentality of the Stranger and Pilgrim. This higher thought process maybe abnormal to the masses, but it is a required mode of operation of a renewed mind and par for the course of salvation. It is an extremely valuable piece to our salvation package and we cannot afford to misunderstand the importance of it. We are not normal, we are peculiar people. We are conscious minded individuals who have the mind of Christ and consider ourselves a stranger and pilgrim to this land.

These all died in faith, not having received the promises, but having seen them afar off, and were persuaded of them, and embraced them, and confessed that they were strangers and pilgrims on the earth ~ Hebrews 11:13

Dearly beloved, I beseech you as strangers and pilgrims, abstain from fleshly lusts, which war against the soul; ~ 1 Peter 2:11

We were never instructed to be like the world but most of us still find ourselves judging the success of our families and vocations by secular standards. Contrariwise, we are instructed to live in this world, but not to become like the world. The world around us thinks totally different than we do and culturally compute daily actions with a different perception. We must be prepared to suffer the persecutions that will come with esteeming others higher than our pride and continue to follow the instructions of the Holy Spirit. When we accept the fact that we should not expect to be accepted, we can have confidence in moving forward without secular validation.

As a youth I can remember reading about men and women of God throughout scripture who did not fit in to modern culture and did not desire to do what the masses did. They were constantly doing what they believed the Father instructed of them and did not worry if it was popular in the culture of their day. When did it become popular amongst the carriers of Light to be just like the world? To operate in this higher thought life we must be settled with the fact that we will not look like the masses. We are required to 'rock the boat' day after day and accept that our plans may suffer a little discomfort. Jesus said, "I come not to make peace, but with a sword". He came to awaken our consciousness and oppose the subconscious LLT processes of the world. It is time to understand that you are a Stranger and Pilgrim to this world. You are a peculiar person that the world will never understand. We are not commanded to try and beat the world at their own game. That does not work for us. Neither are we commanded to get the world to understand and befriend us. Yet many of us are striving to succeed in receiving good judgments from the world and find validation in their approval. Their standards have unknowingly become our measuring stick. We have gained the acceptance of the world but lost our conscious ability to think and operate like Christ.

WHAT'S YOUR RULER?

How do you judge your success? Is it by church attendance? Marital Happiness? Bank Statements? We know the answer should be - none of the above, but the honest truth is that most of our contentment and 'success' is rooted in one or more of those statements. Those called to be Strangers and Pilgrims have become guilty of measuring validation by the convictions of the majority around us. If those around us consider us successful, we believe we really are successful. This is the wrong standard of measurement for a Stranger & Pilgrim. It is extremely limiting and smothers the power and efficacy of our relationship connections. We certainly do not understand the many reasons we are instructed to greet our brothers warmly and intimately. With our limited understanding as humans it may seem foolish and unimportant how we greet people, but we are called to greet each other intimately and to do so in unconditional Love. There are many hearts bound in darkness and the Love of God alone has enough power to break its chains.

I remember the day my wife and I received a phone call from a single mother we were praying for. She was a family friend and told us she was coming over. I was cooking when I heard my wife quickly open the door and rush in. She looked like she had just seen a ghost. She explained that she had just come from the car window of our friend who was now in our driveway, and all she could say was. "Demonic!" Apparently, the enemy tried to attack our friend and was manifesting right at our home. So I began to put down my cooking supplies and walk toward the front door. By this time our friend had also exited her car and was entering the front door of our home. I turned the corner of our hall and just as she was coming in our eyes met and immediately she turned to go the other direction. I called out, "Come here Sis!" She turned around with her hands to her face as if she was bracing for impact as I reached out, wrapped my arms around her and said, "I Love You. Jesus Loves You. All is well..." Immediately, the dark spirit left her, she slowly came to her senses and took a seat.

We have an extremely powerful weapon in the Love of God! We have been giving excuses for decades why we cannot operate in this type of Love life. However, the Bible does not say, "Greet one another with a holy kiss...but only if you live in the Old Testament." We are not excused from seeing our community as Brothers and Fathers and Mothers and Sisters simply because they do not come in a perfect package that our fleshly comfort zone can accept. Yes, body odor is offensive. Attractive people are tempting. Yet none of that changes the Light of Christ nor should it damper the Light that was placed inside you to shine. Make a commitment that you will be a Stranger and Pilgrim to the judgments of this world. Decide that no matter the opinion of the masses, you will Love boldly, shine brightly and allow the comfortable nature of the flesh to be shaken in efforts to walk in the nature of Christ.

DO NOT BE CONFORMED TO THIS WORLD

We cannot be *"conformed to this world, but we must be transformed by renewing our minds"*.   This scripture in Romans 12:2 reveals the command of our Father that we be aware to consciously take action in redeeming our minds from the LLT process of this world. Scripture explains that we are not ignorant to the type of work our adversary uses to gain a foothold against us. He knew that the culture of the world would be set up to conform our minds and capitalize on our subconscious reactive natures. For this reason He left instructions that we should consciously survey the thought process of our minds to remain operating in a higher thought life. Maybe familiarity with this scripture has dampened the efficacy of a higher thought life, but if you decide to take this scripture at face value and really do what it is instructing, this scripture alone would change the course of how you do EVERYTHING in your life.

Let us look at a different passage in Romans the 11th chapter and hear about great men and women of the Faith such as Abraham, Sarah, Moses, Isaac, Jacob, Noah, Joshua and Rahab. Romans 11:13 says, **13 *These all died in faith, not having*** *received the promises, but having seen them afar off were assured of them, embraced them and confessed that they were strangers and pilgrims on the earth.* Think about every feat this great group was responsible for accomplishing throughout scripture. They prophesied to kings and advised many dignitaries of their day, yet they did not seek inclusion, they maintained a stranger and pilgrim mindset. Today we would be hard pressed to find someone with the economic authority of Solomon, or someone like Elijah, that could hear Heaven so clearly that Kings would lose heart upon hearing the words of their mouth.   While this type of authority is uncommon today it is not surprising that also uncommon are those who carry the mentality of the Stranger and Pilgrim.

This mentality goes hand-in-hand with any great exploit of biblical proportions that has been witnessed. Despite all their accolades and the acceptance by the dignitaries and who's who of society, these people remained Strangers and Pilgrims (outcasts).   Today we lack effectiveness on our jobs, in our relationships and in our community largely because the state of our thought process mirrors everybody else. Once we gain stature amongst the elect of society or others of influence, we tend to develop mannerisms we think will help our position and begin to look just like everyone else. Many will even compromise the mind of Christ to preserve their stature in the world, then express justification for their compromise by saying the monies will be used for the kingdom or tithes will greatly increase, but this is not biblical and not at all what is required of us.

We will never be judged on how well secular society accepts us, but on how obedient we were to the assignment. If your goal is the approval and acceptance of the world, carry on with doing whatever it takes to get those of influence to receive you. However, if the goal is to please the heavenly Father, then lose the desire of mass acceptance, walk as a Stranger and Pilgrim and live by faith. If you are called to steward a large asset base or have many lives depending on your success, the process still does not change. Actually, if you steward large assets or lead many, it becomes more imperative to operate as a Stranger and Pilgrim and adopt the higher thought life, as it will give you uncommon insight and boldness to do things the world would never think of.

No matter how big our corporations or congregational followings, there are not many who would come close to the responsibility level of Moses. As a leader, this man was responsible for millions of people, and his promotion happened rather quickly. Not only was he responsible for food and clean drinking water for millions of people almost overnight, but he was also responsible for their safety in a time period where dynasties and kingdoms were formed on the backs of mass murder, enslavement of other nations and controlling the resources of others. The lives of those that followed Moses were consistently at stake and tempers were high. We cannot fathom the sense of responsibility he must have been under to lead this number of people. There was no insurance company or Egyptian government bailout waiting to cover his mistakes. It was do or die every day of leadership. Nonetheless, Moses, with all the power of several million relationships and connections, still considered himself a Stranger and Pilgrim to this world.

This is sobering of mind when we consider that most leaders put in the same position as Moses, would probably be enticed to start their own empire that would last for generations. If a present day leader were handed the type of responsibility and power of Moses, he would first try and receive as much coaching as possible on how to harness his power of influence. He would probably think it 'wisdom' to strive to be a better leader and protect the economic power of his asset base for years to come. *We often feel compelled to use the knowledge and wisdom of the secular world to protect a divine assignment*, but we cannot afford to do that. This may be common to see today, but this is not what the forefathers of faith did. Leaders like Moses actually adopted the mentality of a Stranger and Pilgrim and detached themselves from a culture of leadership pride. In the midst of all of his great exploits Moses kept the

Stranger and Pilgrim mentality and humbled himself. The Bible tells us that, *"... Moses was very humble, above all the men which were upon the face of the earth" – Numbers 12:3.* It would be easy for John the Baptist, clothed in animal skin and maintaining a diet of wild locust and honey to be a Stranger and Pilgrim. His unconventional lifestyle and consecration already made him a stranger of sorts. However, what about the leader of the free world at the time, Moses? What about Abraham, the Father of many nations? Or consider Elijah the prophet and Joseph the dreamer, the second in command of a world empire. Vocationally, these are some of the most notable and coveted positions throughout history, but all these considered themselves Strangers and Pilgrims to the earth. And because of their 'greatness' they kept a detached character that enabled them to make huge impacts for the Kingdom of God. If we desire to make a great impact for the kingdom of God, we must take note of the biblical pattern set by those who have done so before us. It seems we have done less and less with more technology, resource and influence. Maybe we are following a pattern that is logical, acceptable and traditional, but have lost the mentality of the Stranger and Pilgrim. The character of a Stranger and Pilgrim invokes the supernatural resource and divine influence needed to break the chains of bondage over nations. It not only summons the grace and anointing of God

Himself to work on behalf of your assignment, but it also limits the power of the enemy to an experiential plane.

The adversary thrives in the realm of logic, tradition and social acceptance. Things that are 'common' will often lead to familiar footholds of the enemy. Jesus said, "... *for the prince of this world cometh, and hath nothing in me.*" ~ *John 14:30* Our enemy can only claim a foothold on what is familiar to him and things in common within his dark networks. Operating in the mentality of a Stranger and Pilgrim not only releases the power of heaven to work on our behalf, but it also limits the enemy's ability to have access to our lives, thoughts and ministry.

PITFALLS

We all have an innate desire to belong. There is not one of us who grew up longing to be publically criticized and humiliated or talked about. It is not human nature to desire to be apart from the masses. We fellowship in circles with people who think like we do, earn comparable economic benefits and carry the same ideals as we do. Biologically we have a predisposition to develop in packs and our concept of community is based on doing things acceptable to others around us. Our lives have very few Stranger and Pilgrim moments built in by default. We live for comfort and we work hard to make life easier on ourselves and our family. Naturally, we do not want to rock the boat. We do not want to invite discomfort. We would rather allow things to work themselves out than be considered a disruptor. This makes seeking validation so tempting that it could be the most crippling mindset that hinders you from walking as a Stranger and Pilgrim and experiencing the fullness of the life of Christ.

One way to test if you are operating as a Stranger and Pilgrim is to simply take account of your relationships. We know exactly how the world is programmed to react in relationship settings so use this as a barometer to gauge your reflection. How do you operate with loved ones? How do you interact with men or women of the opposite gender? Do you find yourself consistently casting down imaginations? Are you okay with allowing thoughts to settle as long as you do not act on them?

If we take survey of our relationship thought life and objectively examine our interactions with others and see anything but Christ, we need to change our thought process and adopt a higher mindset. We can see it also described in *2 Peter 2:11, 11 Beloved, I beg you as sojourners and pilgrims, abstain from fleshly lusts which war against the soul...* Again we see scripture identify with Strangers and Pilgrims, imploring us to keep from fleshly lusts or, as we have discussed, the lower level processes of thought.   The mind really wants to be comfortable and accept everything that we see in commercials, media and community as acceptable truth.   It is hard work judging everything we allow entrance into our souls. But remember the command is to *'Cast down imaginations and bring every thought into the obedience of Christ' in 2 Corinthians 10:5*. If we are not constantly casting down and capturing our thoughts, we are not operating in the mind of Christ. And when we are not operating in the mind of Christ, we are allowing our worldly circumstances to create the past-files in us that will define our reality. Be the believer who understands the devices of the enemy and lives as a Stranger and Pilgrim to this world. The road is a lot less travelled and consists of a life that is largely anti-self, but it is Christ and the end result is life.

Characteristics of a Stranger and Pilgrim

- *They esteem others higher than their thoughts, their past experiences, and secular definitions.*
- *Think differently than the world and allow the past files of scripture to become the reality.*
- *They treat others as they would like to be treated.*
- *They allow the Light of Christ to shine, especially to others that are in darkness; they do not introvert nor hide.*
- *They care more for the wellbeing of their sister or brother, than they do the desires of the flesh.*

- *They daily place Loving others over all religious traditions of man.*
- *They do not allow the validations of the world to outweigh the character of Christ.*
- *They are confident in standing alone, even if no one around them is able to stand with them* (e.g., when David killed Goliath; no one amongst all of Israel had his same perception of victory).
- *They know that Greater is He that is IN me, than he that is IN the world, as a result, they are strong and courageous.*

You certainly do not find this character amongst the masses, and with good reason. To adopt the mind of Christ it takes conscious effort and detachment from the social norm. We must separate ourselves from the political and ubiquitously accepted mentality of the masses and adopt the mindset of a Stranger and Pilgrim to this world. Strive to think differently every day and adopt a mindset that bases conviction on what is not seen.

Yes, you must become a student of the unseen. The Stranger and Pilgrim consciously reprograms their mind with things not seen around them in the secular world, but instead renews their mind with life occurrences in the word of God. This means that oftentimes our actions and convictions will appear Strange to the natural mind (low level thinking), but we must remember that we are spiritual beings operating under a spiritual mentality, and cannot be judged by any man (1 Corinthians 2:14-15). We must stay in that continual state of consciousness knowing that we are different. We are a Stranger and a Pilgrim in this world. As our past files are rewritten, our actions will become increasing noticeable to those that have a secular mindset. But do not fear, the natural minded man is never expected to understand the mind of Christ, especially when dealing with the opposite gender. Secular programming for physical intimacy between genders is so common that even other believers will often mistake the actions of a Stranger and Pilgrim. While we may have the knowledge of who Christ is and know that we are called to be a Stranger and a Pilgrim, we do not always act on our knowledge. The world is so heavily over sexualized that as we witness and experience more of secular culture around us, it becomes extremely difficult not to submit to its thinking and accept the fact that the world is just bad. The world by nature is dark, and growing worse, but this is the very reason why it is so important for the carriers of Light to strive to do good and not just simply plan and stay away from darkness. No, we must represent a different mentality that does not react to darkness, but pro-acts in Light. As we pro-act in Light, we will exemplify the nature of Christ, and it will not matter how dark the world may be around us.

10

The Church Hug...

Without doubt most believers know that we are called to reach out and minister life to those in darkness, but the age of 'the church hug' is upon us. Unfortunately this mentality is not just in our religious organizations but it has grown outside of the four walls and entered our everyday lives. The 'church hug' can be described as the awkward partial hug you get on a Sunday morning when someone who intends to give you a hug, barely touches you by turning to the side to embrace you with their armpit. It can be one of the most awkward side embraces you encounter. Though well-meaning in its desire to protect patrons of the opposite sex from being tainted with lust, this greeting amongst spiritual family is more suited for the LLT process than the higher thought life. Controversial as this may seem, I believe this practice only shines light on the capacity of darkness and dampens the Light of Christ. Instead of bringing us closer to the mind of Christ it works to enable a consciousness of the powers of darkness, even when darkness is not present. Even if there is no threat, we are still giving a seat to its potential.

The 'church hug' cannot be substantiated with feeling that we need to be more modest in the presence of Jesus in the sanctuary. There is no biblical evidence that Jesus ever demonstrated this practice. If anything, He was condemned for being too close with people and allowing people to be too close to Him. We will have a hard time finding anything in the bible that suggests we should watch out for the adversary in our greetings. Actually the Bible instructs the exact opposite and encourages us to greet one another intimately. Greeting with a 'holy kiss' is mentioned five times in the New Testament. Now, I am not suggesting that we literally kiss everyone we greet every time there is a meeting, but please find encouragement in the Word to be affectionate, and let us learn to purely Love one another in deed when exchanging salutation.

If we were to apply the 'church hug' mentality of operation to the Bible and relegating ministry and intimacy of relationship to same gender dynamics, we would never read about Jesus ministering to, or eating with harlots, adulterers and other women in scripture. In that day eating was not just sitting in close proximity and talking while you both eat your own meal. No, it was much simpler than that. To this day, in developing nations it is common to share meals with others. Eating is viewed more like a covenant practice where there could be one shared cup for beverages, one bread and one plate/bowl, all shared. If you are a 'church hugger' this new visual of Jesus' eating from the same plate as a harlot will probably make you a little nauseous. Throw in the Spirit of God ministering through Elisha to the widow, the Shunamite woman, and rooming in places other women prepared for them, and now in the mind of some, maybe Elisha doesn't seem so holy. The point I am making here is simple. We have really lost sight of the fact that we are recreated Spirits that contain the Light of God and the mind of Christ. This is the mindset in which the bible is written. This has not changed over the years to accommodate darkness. We must remain encouraged to walk boldly in Light, not in the darkness of fear.

Leadership

Leaders, we should be careful about our labels of wisdom. Our definitions of wisdom may not always be quantifiably black and white. We should take careful consideration of how we speak to those under our stewardship that our personal convictions are not received as direct commands from the Lord. The Father brings people from many different backgrounds and experiences. Sometimes where you as a leader may be weak, another may be strong. Christ is our goal, so everything we do should pave a pathway to becoming more like Him regardless of our shortcomings. The danger is when we use experiences from our personal life to make far reaching judgments that cause our personal convictions to become law. For a long time we have been preaching messages birthed from pain and disappointment. This has its place and can render wonderful revelations birthed from our sharing. However a Stranger and Pilgrim mentality also means that we are not like those who bequeathed the pain but we are striving to keep others from pain. We are to remain focused on Christ and liberating people into the Light and intimacy of Him, which is the only way to truly heal.

For example, many may believe that wisdom says driving 65mph is more dangerous than driving 25mph. The pain of a past crash may actually keep some people from flying or driving on the freeway altogether. That is a choice of restraint because of their past experiences, and it is their choice to make. The problem arises when a person in leadership spreads a yoke of personal experience as law. We are all striving to simply look more like Christ. Regardless of where we or others may have fallen short, the nature and liberty of Christ and His recreated spirit in us should likewise be the goal and subsequent law.

Imagine the limitations of the mindset that says, 'We do not necessarily **fear** driving 65mph, but you can die or crash, so there is wisdom in driving slower; therefore we should not drive on the freeway!' While it indeed may be true that you can die driving 65mph, it does not mean a yoke-binding law should now be imposed on parishioners limiting them from driving on the freeway. Personal experience is not be the best type of supporting evidence on which to establish general laws of restraint, especially when those laws limit the mind of Christ. Unfortunately, we have done this with our viewpoints of flesh, sexualization of the opposing gender and positive intimacy.

We have allowed darkness to completely condemn the Light because of our past failed experiences. We can no longer afford to allow our wide path failures to hinder our narrow path victories. If we continue to do this, we will duplicate another generation that is more geared towards the fear of destruction rather than the victory of the narrow path and difficult way. In our wake, instead of liberating captives by reaching outside of our ability, we are in danger of building prisons of condemnation and complicated lower level thought processes. If we fail to repent from the fear of flesh, we are in danger of repeating the same condemning judgments of the scribes and Pharisees that crucified the Messiah. Let us remember that the Gentiles were not the perpetrators of the crucifixion. It was the keepers of law, the phylactery experts and councils that condemned Jesus. It mattered not that He was doing the works of the Father and fulfilling prophesy. The fruit of His work were captives set free, and multitudes were healed and inspired to peace; which is why when they took up stones to kill Him, He said, *"Many good works have I showed you from my Father; for which of those works do you stone me?" The Jews answered him, saying, "For a good work we stone you not; but for blasphemy; and because that you, being a man, make yourself God." - John 10: 32-33*

This is the response you will receive when you walk in higher processes of thought. Ridicule and rebuke will come. It will not matter that as a result of you shining the Light of Christ, people are being changed and eating from the fruits of the spirit in operation of your life. Since your actions do not line up with the traditional rules of man and the generally accepted mentality of the masses, then you can expect to be wrongfully judged. One of my mentors used to echo a statement that has since been my principle fallback when I receive abrasive judgment from those that should be a support. She would say, "The hardest thing to do is to win the lost (secular world) without offending the saved (the church)." I never fully understood that statement until I entered the mission field and began seeing ministry being conducted without the traditions and yokes of men added. I witnessed great supernatural exploits when there was focused attention on pleasing the Father without care about how darkness viewed them.

We do not need to concern ourselves with the voice of distractors when fulfilling vision and operating in purpose. Sometimes the same spirit that came upon David's brothers, as he pondered fighting Goliath, will come upon your peers. At these times we must remember; **what** we are: Spirit, **who** we are called to: The Lost, and **what** is in us: His Light. When we adopt this mentality and start living to reach outside the comforts of self and traditional rules of man, we will begin to hear the voice of truth speaking clearly to our heart through scripture.

If you desire to be transformed from simply complying with traditional rules of man, to actually fulfilling the great commission and deeply touching those around you, you must also leave the validations of man and walk boldly the path of Stranger & Pilgrim. This mindset will open the door to great exploits. Much like Joseph, those who have been misused and abused even by their own families will operate in the capacity of forgiveness even when it is in their authority to silently enact vengeance. David, divinely crowned King, yet voluntarily remained in service to the current authority although the King attempted to murder him. Elijah would speak and the King would tremble, but even in all his power, he subjected himself to a voice that instructed him to wait by a brook and be fed from the mouth of a regurgitating raven. Most of us today would rebuke such voices. If we were internally honest, we would do so because those type of instructions do not immediately benefit us, and do not look like success.

We have learned to give, to receive. We sow, to reap. We pray, to get answers... Right? What about Giving to just be a blessing? Sowing to cultivate? Or praying to simply intercede for someone or communicate our Love to our Father? Time and again we hear messages that promote self and reinforce an anti-Christ mind. This is highly damaging to the instructions of Strangers and Pilgrims. We cannot think like this and experience the fullness of the treasure inside our earthen vessel. Our mindset may be foolish to a low level thinker and natural minded man, but we should expect that type of judgment. So do not lose heart. Embrace the mind of Christ with confidence. Be empowered to Love boldly those around you and see the fruits of the spirit in abundant manifestation.

The Power of Love in Action:

During the time my wife and I were courting we wrote many letters to one another and had long phone conversations. One evening during a phone conversation between she and I, this presence of Love just filled my heart. I mean, it was so evident that I told her that I had to go hug somebody. Now, it was probably past midnight at this time but I didn't care. I lived in

an area where there was always somebody outside, and I could
not contain what was inside. It felt like a burning fire that was
not necessarily hot with heat, but with purpose. So, we ended
our phone conversation and I walked out to the main street
about a block away from my house. I did not see anyone
immediately and remember just thanking the Lord, not really
knowing what to do. When I looked up again I saw a woman
coming down the road. I didn't know her or her occupation but
I greeted her with a, "Hey Sis, how you doing? You know Jesus
Loves you?" I really didn't expect an answer, I think I really just
wanted to find a lead in to a hug :) She said a few words and as
we parted I reached to give her a hug. She looked a little
surprised and after one or two seconds released her arms.
Well...I did not. I squeezed even more tightly and though my
spirit was yelling loudly with purpose, I just softly told her she
was loved. "Jesus loves you Sis! He loves you so much." I said.
After a few moments I felt a sort of jerking motion. By this time
my burden was leaving so my mind was now thinking, 'Did I go
too far? Is she jerking away? Maybe I should let go now.' So I
released her and found that she was not jerking away but tears
were running down her cheeks and she was crying
uncontrollably. I embraced her again until we finally parted
ways and I walked home thankful that the Father would use me.

Beloved, by this they will know. The message of the gospel is
about letting the Light of Christ shine in dark places. We are

here to serve. We need to release our inhibition and lower level secular mindsets. Be free to walk in the power of the Love of Christ, in Jesus name. God is Love and you are His Light that was created to shine all over the world. We do not allow darkness to dictate when or how we Love. We are commanded and commissioned by the Creator of all things to GO. So, go forth and Love all nations without inhibition. You are here to heal the broken hearted and set captives in bondage free. Do not be ashamed, you are needed.

You are a Medic...

11

We Are the Medics

Life certainly has a tendency to be quite difficult at times. When dealing with so much personal pain, it can be hard to consider others. However, thinking of others and esteeming them higher than ourselves actually activates our faith. The phrase, *'higher than ourselves'* means that we literally put the well-being of others above our own fleshly desires and comforts. This is especially true when dealing with those of opposing genders. We cannot truly say that we Love others if we are reacting to them with disdain or lustful desire.

The goal of every interaction with others should be that we leave them better than the state in which we found them. When a woman meets a man and befriends him, the end result of her interaction with him should leave him desiring to be a better son, better brother, better husband, and/or father. Likewise, when a man befriends a woman, when she leaves his presence, she should be more equipped to be a better daughter, better sister, better wife and/or mom. We cannot equip each other to be better people if we follow the cultural pattern and thought process of the masses.

The secular world communicates that when there is attraction between two persons of opposing genders, that Eros or an erotic type of physical interaction is the end goal. But we know that Eros love is not the highest form of Love, nor is it the closest type of intimacy. Jesus said, *"Greater love hath no man than this, that a man lay down his life for his friends."* ~ **John 15:13** The Love we operate in and demonstrate daily is not self-serving upon our own lusts. It seeks to esteem others higher than our fleshly desires and passion. This is often difficult to digest because of the many secular past-files we have stored away in our consciousness, but even as you read this book you are replacing past-files and renewing the mind against the tenets of social acceptance.

Remember, the highest form of Love has never been erotic in nature. This is hard to truly comprehend since 98% of what we experience of Love in songs, movies, TV and marketing is Erotic and sexual in nature. However, the Bible explains that the highest form of Love is the ability for someone to lay down their life for a friend. If we are attracted to someone and truly Love them that is great. We should feel free to operate in Love with them; and refuse to operate according to the desires of flesh. However, since the passion and desire of flesh is so heavily advertised and enticing, a lot of the world is trapped. Trapped by what we believe we should do and trapped by the function we believe our body parts and genitalia play in serving our flesh.

Our bodies were made for purposes greater than passion and more valuable than Eroticism. Men have more testosterone, this hormone creates more muscle mass, chiseled frames and a hunger to conquer. Men were made to provide, cultivate and protect community and loved ones. A chiseled frame is very appealing to the eyes, we are not saying that the flesh does not exist. No. Quite frankly you cannot ignore this elephant in the room and operate in the mind of Christ. However, when you recognize the purpose of the elephant in room, it becomes less of a taboo avoidance and more of an instrument of purpose. For instance when men, who are genetically predisposed to produce more muscle than their female counterpart, learn that their attributes were given to provide, cultivate and protect loved ones, they can begin to interact with a nature that seeks to operate in those attributes.

Subsequently, women who are genetically predisposed to produce hormones that form nourishing mammary glands also possess emotional palates fit to nurture. These attributes are in stark contrast to their male counterparts. Our Father God is also referred to as El Shaddai, which in Hebrew means 'All Breasted', 'Nourisher' or 'Sustainer'. If we take a look at that definition alone we can find the target of the enemy is to get us to look away from our created nature, and devalue it with sexual manipulation. We need to rewrite how we view ourselves and the world around us. We have been bewitched in how we view our brothers and sisters and it is affecting more areas of our lives than we think. The more we see Eros and sexual intimacy around us, the more we began to believe in its supremacy over our higher Agape forms of interaction. We carry life and like Jesus, we were created to walk as if we have healing in our wings.

The Battle of Life

Our relationships are filled with battles that we endure. Some of these battles are an all-out war, while others are mild disagreements. We all defend our positions in our relationship battles differently. Some take a spiritual stand, while others battle physically and mentally but the point remains; we all battle just the same. Everyday a new challenge arises for us to overcome. Within these conflicts we experience both victory and defeat. The longer we live, the wiser we become and we can begin to see both outcomes as growth.

However, something happens during the times when we are deeply wounded in battle. The times where though we fought well, we were blindsided and wounded by our circumstances. It is here that we find ourselves cut, battered and bleeding because we were not able to properly defend ourselves or quite simply were just defeated by an opposing force. Though we may try and hide our wounds with putting on fake expressions and holding politically correct conversations with our peers, we cannot deny the fact that everyone battles and so everyone is wounded at some point in life. How many times do we simply pass by people not realizing their hurts, or their daily or lifetime battles? Although we realize that our economies are failing, our health and marriages are failing, churches are losing credibility and there are famines, earthquakes and natural disasters all over the world, we still have not fully come to the realization that there will probably never be a better time to recognize the wounded than the present. When do we start to recognize those that are in pain and carry the deep wounds of life's battles? They are the ones that actually need what we so compellingly confess that we embody but often fail to demonstrate in our daily action. We call ourselves 'spiritual' and 'awakened' because we give to charitable organizations and donate our gently used treasures, however we still find it hard to step outside our schedules and family obligations to esteem someone else higher than our personal concerns. We see death and destruction and utter moral decay both domestically and abroad, yet consumerism and tainted imagery continue to shape our process of thought about our neighbors, our wives, husbands, family and friends.

This is the time when the 'House of God' should be the most empathetic and loving, but contrariwise we have become the representation of those who just judge. We can no longer operate as a generation that reads the Word and attends church simply to find out how right we are. It is not acceptable to pass self-righteous convictions off as 'godly judgment' on others who are wounded and in darkness. When the wounded are broken in life's most tumultuous battles and in need of life, we are oftentimes found speaking more judgment than life.

Be honest, ask yourself how many times you have heard that someone has fallen into sin and you immediately judge why it happened and where they were at fault? Our idea of help has been to provide scripture guide lines to what they need to change to make it better. At some point correction will be absolutely necessary, but even the most natural man knows what is needed when his fellow soldier breaks rank, runs into enemy territory and is wounded and left for dead. He may be disappointed, he may be shocked, he may be rightfully upset that he has to stop his assignment to care for the disobedient and now wounded, but when he sees his fellow soldier (*whether he knows him well or not*) wounded, bleeding and moaning in pain, even the most natural and self-centered person knows who to call...

A Medic.

Instead of realizing our God given assignments to bring comfort as well as correction, we as the body of Christ have been guilty of blatant insensitivity. Time after time we see family, friends, and strangers who are regular people, falling down overtaken, noticeably wounded and in need of attention. Instead of being the medic that is needed, believers gather around and cut them again and again with our (s)words. Meaning, our words become as swords and our comforting words of 'wisdom' become comfortless piercings of pride and fear. Can you imagine a soldier stumbling upon a wounded comrade and indignantly proceeding to shout orders for his comrade to get it together?

"Hey, I know you cannot see and have a fatal wounds to your head and chest... and...and WOW! I see BOTH your legs are broken and you're losing a lot of blood from your carotid artery but, hey, get up! Get up and arm yourself soldier! Hold your head high! That will teach you to walk that close to the mine field...Rookie!!!"

If any soldier acted this way, we would think that soldier seriously lacked empathy or was facing some type of debilitating war trauma. This certainly would not be considered the norm especially if he carries the title of a medic. Unfortunately, this is the mentality believers have adopted in dealing with the wounded today. We have many believers that do not carry themselves like they have a relationship with the beliefs and the God they talk so much about. We have become so affixed on helping ourselves and coming out of our personal challenges, that we have abandoned the understanding of how to judge purely and biblically.

For instance, when a young teen gets pregnant, or the new convert is caught gambling, or the deacon loses his temper in a meeting and is revealed as imperfect, instead of providing a haven of relief and healing in word and in deed, we are often found emboldened in self-righteousness and find ourselves taking the stance of judge and jury, instead of protector. We must gain understanding in this area and know that certain wounds will not allow for immediate movement or change. When one is wounded, perhaps recovery is needed more than a recital of what is wrong in their life. Once we realize this and we are open to seeing properly, we can correctly empathize with those we are called to nurture with the fruits of the Spirit in Galatians 5:22 and not pass self-righteous judgment on others out of our wounded hearts. Rather, we now become the friend that sticks closer than a brother and learn to esteem our brother or sister higher than ourselves. We can place others higher than ourselves by simply being there for them. We may not understand their trapped position, but we are called to nurse them back to health with empathy and Agape

Love. Now this approach may not be needed ALL the time, however, another sword of judgment is rarely the prescription. It may just be that some nurturing and a little dose of forgiveness that is able to heal and restore life is just what the Great Doctor ordered. Beloved, let us truly <u>LOVE</u> one another...

12

Partner Perspective

Keeping the medic principle in mind, envision this: *An EMT is arriving on the scene of an accident where a mother and her 3 kids have just been hit by an oncoming car. Taking a quick survey of the scene, the Emergency Medical Technician knows he has the training, experience and mind to bring the potential lifesaving assistance to the victims; a mother and her 3 kids. As he is exiting the ambulance he gathers himself and the instruments needed to administer the medical aide but as he comes closer he notices something and...he stops. Upon further examination, he realizes that the victim is a woman and he is a happily married man. To not jeopardize his own marriage, he decides to not engage the mother of 3 and wait for another credentialed technician of the same gender to arrive on scene.*

This may sound utterly ridiculous to you. Maybe you feel that this EMT quite frankly needs a change of vocation, but this is exactly what our reaction to darkness looks like. If the victim was your sister, mother or daughter, you would not be concerned about the physical gender or sexual orientation of the technician. This probably would never cross the thought process of a sober minded individual. Our primary concern would be the lifesaving aide administered by the qualified EMT not their gender, race or creed. In actuality, it would matter not if they were a PhD, MD or skilled passerby, we would hope someone would offer help and provide any assistance that would save the life of our loved ones. This concept is easy to digest when it comes to administering medical care but when we consider ourselves administering the Light of Christ to those in darkness, it somehow becomes an entirely different understanding.

We who carry the Light of Christ should understand to a greater degree that the spirit of man is of much more importance than gender. *"There is neither Jew nor Greek, there is neither bond nor free, there is neither male nor female: for ye are all one in Christ Jesus." ~* **Galatians 3:28** We are often ensnared by allowing fleshly dictates to govern our spiritual assignments. According to scripture we should be operating more in the spirit of Christ and not limiting ministry of eternal life to physical attributes, background or status. While we as believers ponder fleshly limitation, our natural minded counterparts are not pausing and second guessing themselves when it comes to administering care to those in need. They engage without respect to physical attributes, attraction or distraction. We must change this mentality and understand the truth about who we are. Above all else, we are *Spirit* beings that contain the *Light* of Christ.

Any mindset that seeks to destroy that value is anti-Christ. When we continue to operate according to the dictates of natural limitation we will see the power of our witness and ministry weakened and limited to physical measures. There is too much entrusted to us to stop at the darkness of flesh. Change must come and we must embrace who we are truly called to be.

Never limit your Light based on the failures of another man. As a minister, my earthly dad always would say, "Never bring the word of God *down* to the level of another man's experience." A powerful statement because oftentimes we do this exact thing. We can use the experiences of others to bring us up, as ultimately Christ is the goal. But we should never limit the word of God and its truth to the personal experiences and failures of others. The Bible tells us that we are equipped to do greater works than Jesus, but we are often comparing ourselves to other fallen men. That is like trying to paint a completely supernatural portrait using paint from Home Depot. It is not possible. If we desire a supernatural picture, we need to use supernatural attributes. **We cannot say that Jesus is the goal, all while limiting ourselves to the failures of Uncle Jim or Pastor such and such.**

Break free from those limitations! Go forth and *serve!* You must begin to inquire of the Lord just what the nature of Christ in you is capable of, or why you have it. Once you understand why you have the Light of Christ in you, you will understand that *you* do not *choose* whom to give it to. When a light switch is turned ON in a room it does not choose to shine in one place but not in another. We are instructed to "Let our Light shine!" We can only be obedient to the instructions and examples already laid before us in scripture. No place in scripture are we instructed to allow sexual gender or orientation or potential darkness to dictate how the gospel is shared. This may be even more difficult ministry for the married, but not because of the sanctity of marriage. No. Actually the sanctity of marriage provides the perfect anchor to minister with support and understanding from another vantage point. It is an advantage to have a supportive anchor physically, mentally and emotionally when interceding on behalf of others and taking on bombardments of enemy fire.

Ministering from the relational position of marriage is most ideal when operating in the Love of Christ. It is most challenging when we relate to our partners improperly and allow unbiblical beliefs to have preeminence. Some of these reasons were expressed by Paul in 1 Corinthians 7. Paul felt an unction to share the vantage point of being completely single and separate from a life partner. Though the Father was not giving this as a commandment, he says in verse 6, he found it pertinent to share what he believes.

*"But I speak is by permission, and not of command-
ment. For I would that all men were even as I myself. But
every man hath his proper gift of God, one after this
manner, and another after that. I say therefore to the
unmarried and widows, It is good for them if they abide
even as I. But if they cannot contain, let them marry: for it
is better to marry than to burn ~ 1 Corinthians 7: 6-9*

Paul's belief when it comes to married partners and ministry
is not of commandment, but he does describe how those who
are married have to battle another layer of lower level
thinking. He was expressing that from his vantage point, it
was better to not have to deal with it at all. This is logical, but
since Paul had never experienced a God ordained marriage
working properly when he wrote this, it is simply his opinion
based on human LLT. Ministry is high level outward giving.
The very nature of ministry is depleting of self and esteeming
others higher, and so this type of Agape ministry can be
challenging in the eyes of a partner especially when the office
of marriage is largely possessive in nature. This possessive
nature is actually what Paul is describing throughout this 7th
chapter but we will pick up at verse 32-34.

*... He that is unmarried careth for the things that belong to
the Lord, how he may please the Lord: But he that is
married careth for the things that are of the world, how he*

*may please his wife. There is difference also between a wife and a virgin. **The unmarried woman careth for the things of the Lord, that she may be holy both in body and in spirit: but she that is married careth for the things of the world, how she may please her husband. ~ I Corinthians 7:32-34***

It is generally assumed that the married man or woman has the highest obligation to their spouse. We are not owners of ourselves when we join in marriage. We become co-laborers with our spouse and joint partners in everything and become one flesh.   This means, that we now *must* take into consideration the feelings, desires, wants, needs and countenance of our partner.   On the surface, this makes ministry as a married couple highly difficult, especially when it comes to cross-gender ministry, friendships and relationships of the opposite sex. I have heard of marital partners so deeply enthralled with one another, that they forbid any friendship outside of their union. Some may argue the healthiness of that arrangement, but I am not writing to condemn anyone. I am simply sharing the obstacles married partners face in fulfilling the Great Commission and how you can reprogram the LLT process of the world especially when dealing with the opposite sex.

Example: *There are many times that my wife is called to minister to someone outside the home. Even though her assignment did not concern me directly, I began to feel a direct attack from the enemy. I mean, it was not me who had the marital problem or facing diagnosis with a chronic illness, but somehow I felt the pressure and burden of a weight pushing against her assignment. Somehow the enemy was making her assignment away from home, a marital problem at home. I would feel like she was spending too time much with them. I would feel jealous of time spent. Insecurity of my position. The enemy literally threw the laundry basket of dirty darts to make the home environment unstable and so uncomfortable that anything surrounding outside ministry just seemed burdensome. It did not matter whether the person she was ministering to was male or female. The darts just kept coming until I was conscious to rehearse who she is and what exactly we are called to do in the lives of others. I would ask myself, "Are we called to simply have an above average marriage, or are we called to people?" Once the perspective was corrected, the chain of thoughts switched to support of her assignment in prayer instead of giving audience to the adversary.*

Our enemy is not ignorant. As much as we would like to call him a complete idiot, he is really not a fool at all. He is smart and cunning, and we do ourselves a disservice when we do not take him seriously. ***If we had half the discipline and work ethic of our enemy, we would be much further along in our spiritual walk.*** The only characteristic that makes him a huge target for the label 'fool', was and always will be his pride. To think that he could dethrone I AM, as the creator and ruler of all things simply because of his intelligence and cunning was not intelligent and he is still paying for acting and believing those thoughts. Satan was so prideful in his intellect and beauty that he believed the created could overthrow the Creator!

We may think it foolish to think along these lines, but it is not such a farfetched idea when we consider how much instruction we receive from the Father yet we still do the opposite simply because of what our pride thinks is right or good. Scripture states that we should do *nothing* out of selfish ambition but instead consider the position of others over our own. How many times a day do we consider others over ourselves? Take a moment... How many times a day? And this is not just our immediate family. Who of us can say that their life is based on this scripture and nothing anyone says will change that? If we had more believers living lives based on scripture, the impact of our character would shake the nations at the core! Instead, we have been unsuccessful in reaching the lost. We fail time and time again when we allow those darts from the enemy to feed our low level thought processes that embolden reactionary mindsets rooted in flesh. This is how we become that spouse that causes disagreement before, during and/or after ministry. Indirectly, the enemy is using us to hinder our partner. The enemy knows that he may not always have a direct path to the one that is stepping outside themselves, because they are not overly concerned with their own desires but rather, moving forward in ministry to engage and touch the lives around them. When we become the marital partner that is not mindful to keep away from actions and beliefs of selfish ambition, we enter into a lower level thought process that allows our adversary to experience victory after victory.

We will not always know what the enemy is up to. We will not always realize that as a result of our forbidding our partner to engage ministry, either same gender or not, that we are actually playing into the hand of the enemy and causing the Light of ministry to be hidden. Again, our enemy rarely comes with a pitchfork and horns. Meaning, he rarely looks like a bad deal. Rather he disguises himself as an angel of Light. No one really desires to sin, but we do sin when we try too hard to do things on our own.

Adam and Eve did not know they were blatantly rebelling. They were deceived into thinking that there was a new and better way to have dominion and fulfill their assignment. They thought, 'If I am supposed to have dominion, then having the knowledge of what is good or what is evil is certainly not a bad thing to possess...Right?!' We now know this was a raw deal because we see the aftermath of that decision and must live with the repercussions of it daily. Though Adam and Eve were only trying to help and preserve the assignment, they were trying outside the prescriptions of the Father, so they experienced defeat. Much like we experience defeat in the power of our witness and marital relationships when we try to preserve our marriages and relationships outside the word of God. Our partner position is exalted above His word when we fail to, '*Do nothing out of selfish ambition, but rather esteem others higher than yourselves.*' -Phil 2:3. Yet, we subscribe to the mentality that since we are married we should always have first rights to our spouses. Everyone else must get behind our desires and needs.

If we took an honest audit of our demands and requests of our partners we would see that most of those requests are birthed out of selfish ambition without regard to the preference of another over ourselves. The perspective we have about our partner is almost always, 'me first', through the eyes of selfish ambition. There are stories I can share of the many close relationships my wife and I have had in different seasons of our life. Some friends who are very close to us have followed paths that led to darkness simply as a result of trying to preserve themselves and failing to esteem others higher. Their pathways to destruction are so similar that we can now recognize these patterns and can almost predict what others will experience if they do not turn away. This has uncanny accuracy because the tactics of the enemy are so effective that he rarely changes the ambush. He is actually using the same tactics he used in the Garden and is still pulling the veil over our eyes and getting very good returns. Here are a few patterns and devices of the devil:

Step 1 – A seed of Void is planted. You begin feeling lack. As if there is a void that needs to be filled. We have all battled with personal desires and wants. 'The grass is always greener on the other side'. This is human nature. So the enemy uses this nature to poison his darts.

 ❖ "I am missing something."
 ❖ "Something in my life, is not right."
 ❖ "Something in my marriage is not right"

***IN THE GARDEN.** (Satan used the same tactic with Adam and Eve):"There is something in your assignment of dominion that I need, and I do not have it."*

These are all normal, everyday feelings and emotions that we are subjected to regardless of our marital status. However, these normal feelings and desires become poisonous when we begin to accept them as truth. After all, who said you were in void and in need of something else? Did this feeling come from the Holy Spirit or are you simply dealing with a dart? Remember counterfeit feelings? If you do not cast down this imagination we will suffer greatly. *Always, always consider the origin of the dart, thought or emotion.* This is called a stage of presentment of void. Once the presentment is made, he then needs to water the seed.

Step 2 -He waters the seed. The Bible is pretty clear that we need to cast down imaginations and for good reason. When we allow any seed or thought to remain without consciously taking authority over its presence we give the enemy a place on the canvas of our minds. He now has a seed in us that has not been cast down, and he can simply water it to cause it to take root. The voice of the enemy will water the seed of darkness by playing to your 'void' and self-preservations and enlarging the barren feelings and emotional despair caused by your perceived lack.

❖ "Yes, you SHOULD have this, but you don't…"
❖ "You, DESERVE attention."
❖ "Actually, you were never really in Love. They are not your soul mate, this is your soul mate."

IN THE GARDEN. (Here is Satan watering the seed placed in Adam's head): **"As one to whom God gave dominion, you SHOULD be able to at least discern Good from Evil Adam."**

Step 3 –**We take mental possession; it's Harvest time.**
After *accepting* these common darts of despair or lack, we
actually give life to them in the incubator of our minds. The
key here is where the thought or feeling originated. Again, our
enemy will most likely never come with pitchfork, horns and
breathing fire of doom through his nostrils. This is too
blatantly obvious and we will abort the proposed mission.
However, with all the self-help publications, seminars and
subliminal messages, it is easy to feel uneasy about any
uncomfortable situation. So when we choose to accept the
dart of darkness, a void is created and over time it is watered,
it has taken root and now the viewpoint of our enemy has
grown into our own belief. The thoughts change to
accommodate selfish ambition and now everything is about
ME or 'I'.

 ❖ "I can HAVE a different life."
 ❖ "I DESERVE a different life."
 ❖ "My partner should be about ME"

IN THE GARDEN.(The thoughts of Adam and Eve): **"Yes, the**
tree IS good for ME, pleasant to my eyes and will make ME
wise."

Step 4 - **We take action.** Now that the proposed seed of
darkness is embraced, our mind confirms this reality. Our
mind now tells us that we are obligated to correct the injustice

or inadequacy. As a result, we feel emboldened to take these calculated actions based on this belief. These actions will manifests as:

- ❖ ADULTERY
- ❖ PROHIBITING PARTNER TO BE A LIGHT
- ❖ DIVORCE

IN THE GARDEN. BOTH ADAM AND EVE ATE FROM THE TREE OF KNOWLEDGE IN DIRECT DISOBEDIENCE

This tactic is so old that the enemy used it in the Garden of Eden and is still using it with uncanny success to this day. Many decisions we make and many perspectives we have are not rooted in spiritual insight or truth, but rather they are seeds of darkness that we should have cast down at the inception. So how do we do that? Let me share some real life situations that make most people who read them cringe inside just thinking about the red flags.

Practical Situation:

A believing woman encounters another lady at a store. There is an attraction there for various reasons (remember the spirit is the greatest attraction). This time there are shoes the believing woman is wearing that the lady just happens to like, so she compliments her and the two dialogue in conversation vacillating from fashion, to family and athletics. Through dialogue, the believing woman feels led (by the spirit) that this lady may need more than just a 10min conversation in the grocery store. They exchange information and through text and conversation decide to connect for coffee later the following week. As a result of the initial attraction the believing woman is able to allow the Father to use her time, experience and openness to hear His voice and the life of the lady is changed forever. The lady is encouraged in her marriage. She sees the error of certain habits and is greatly encouraged in her walk and intimacy with the Lord.

That is a practical situation that most of us have been in and probably have similar stories. There is not much higher level thought or going against the grain of society here. Most can understand exactly how this happens. Your local church body would probably congratulate the woman and say that this represents Christ and many angels are rejoicing in the heavens. However, what if the story changes and instead of meeting a lady at the grocery store, *the believing woman* meets a man?

Practical Situation (cross-gender)

A believing woman encounters a gentleman at the store. There is an attraction there for various reasons (remember the spirit is the greatest attraction). This time the young man just happens to like the shoes the believing woman is wearing so he compliments her and the two dialogue in conversation vacillating from fashion, to family and athletics. Through dialogue, the believing woman feels led (by the spirit) that this gentleman may need more than just a 10min conversation in the grocery store. They exchange information and through text and conversation decide to connect for coffee later. As a result of the initial 'attraction', the believing woman is able to allow the Father to use her time, experience and openness to hear His voice and the life of this man is changed forever. The man is encouraged in his marriage. He sees the error of certain habits and is greatly encouraged in his walk and intimacy with the Lord.

Now most of us read this practical example are squirming inside and already protesting. "NO! This is not right. It is an *abomination*. Something is wrong here. It just does not sit right." We feel that in this scenario there is too much at stake and if a member of the local church body would see this, they would probably not think good thoughts about you nor encourage you by saying you represented Christ. For most believers, it is too dangerous and unwise.

The goal is not to be completely vulnerable with, open to and recklessly free with every one of the opposite sex, but we must model Christ here. What did Christ do when he met the woman at the well? Social acceptances of the day made it abnormal for a man to even talk to a woman in public, even if it was his own wife. Jesus was not so concerned about social normalcy and tradition that the Light within Him took a back seat. Now some may reason, "But, that is 'Jesus'! Of course He should minister to whomever He wants. He is the Son of God." It would be a travesty to deprive someone of experiencing the Son of God simply because of a social culture of tradition that frowned upon cross gender interaction. In the same manner, we are the present children of God. We carry the Spirit of Christ. What He did, we are to do. We should only seek to make the will of the Father known to everyone we come in contact with. Again, ask yourself; could we have missed the mark as it relates to the credence we give to physical traits? Should physical attributes govern our ministry Light? Are we hearing the voice of the Holy Spirit when we engage the opposite sex, or are we simply hiding our Lights because of Fear? Have we allowed the Holy Spirit room to operate as Jesus did with the women at the well, or do the confines of marriage supersede that type of ministry? Lastly, could this mentality be crippling our ministry to others and dampening our impact?

It may be extremely difficult to provide an objective answer, especially if we are not creating new past files of positive intimacy. Problems arise when our identity is not wholly founded in Christ. We begin to pull from experiences of sexualization witnessed in cinema, TV etc., and begin to fail to see ourselves as Light first. We consistently see ourselves as flesh first, even before we see ourselves as spirit. Sexual gender is not the main problem when it comes to ministry, *perspective* is. When we walk conscious of who we are and what we have in us, our perspective changes.

The proper way to capture the dissatisfaction with the cross-gender scenario above is to acknowledge the source of your disdain. Is the Christ in you saying this is too much, or is LLT telling you that it is just wisdom to avoid this scenario? Where does the source of your concern come from? What is the end result of your actions? Does it allow your Light to shine or cause you to hide your Light? Who gets the glory from your actions? Lastly, whom are you trying to please? Answer these questions and I am sure the light bulb of a higher though life will start to glow.

As the husband of the type of wife that is led of the Spirit to minister to anyone regardless of race, gender or creed, I feel the perspective of the partner is of equal importance in ministry. If we do not learn how to consciously cast down imaginations and let loose the possessive nature of marriage, we will be in bondage to fleshly limitation. Not only will our ministry and impact on others suffer, but our daily interactions will also be open to a wide barrage of lower level thinking darts. Contrary to logical opinion, when we do not operate in the higher thought processes and Love like Christ without regard to gender or other physical limitation, we are more susceptible to fall in our relationships.

One night while reading Ezekiel 33:8 the conviction of the Holy Spirit set in. God sent warnings of judgment to the watchman of Israel, Ezekiel at the time. If Ezekiel did not minister the warning, the blood of the offending sinner would be required of him. In my conviction, I realized that we are all present day watchmen. We are carriers of the Light. We are on post and looking out for the enemy, for the return of Christ, for signs of the times and much more. We are our brother's keeper and should not fail to deliver the Light of Christ, who is a form of warning and a true message of liberty. Like Ezekiel, we are watchmen I believe we enter into a degree of judgment that will require blood on our hands if we do not complete our assignment.

In marriage, both partners are watchmen. Though they may have separate assignments at times, there is joint reward and responsibility. When we inhibit the assignment of our spouse, we are also in danger of having the blood of those who needed the ministry required on our hands. Again, we may carry separate assignments, but joint reward and responsibility.

We need to release our partners to let their Light shine and grow together in grace. The Father place much weight on our physical makeup or gender in ministry. There is no scriptural excuse for not allowing your partner to witness to that lady in line, or letting their Light shine on that gentleman at the store simply because they were a different gender. These are the kind of rules that actually do not promote spiritual growth and certainly, do not promote the kingdom. These rules have caused us to hide our relationship Light in introversion. Marriage is a partnership that should shine the brightest and have the most support in Agape ministry but we have allowed possessive selfish ambition to dampen our witness.

Lose the selfish ambition and possessive nature that dampens the Light of your marriage. Our partnerships are a Light to a dark world. The roles we play in the development of one another is very important. My wife and I both had to change our perspective on ministry for Christ to be fully demonstrated through the life of our family. We often talk for hours about the various ministry opportunities and the dark darts and thoughts that accompany them. We share our experiences to fortify our minds and better understand the nature of the battles we face. We realize the enemy absolutely hates the witness and Light of Christ. Satan cannot stand our freedom in Christ. Nor can he stomach the fact that the Father can use us at any time, to minister to anybody, no matter their physical earthly package.

I have experienced many attractive women tell me that I am the only man that looks them in the eye when we talk. Since they are attractive women with God given talents of physique or beauty, they get a lot of fleshly attention. Many have tried to seek purity and come to church but describe how the men in church 'tuck their tails' and actually shy away from them. Unfortunately, these men are trying so hard to avoid darkness that they never think about embracing this lady as a Sister and considering her greater good first. So on one hand these women are verbally mistreated and looked at as eye candy by the men in the secular world. On the other hand, they are totally avoided and do not experience the Light of Christ or brotherly Love from those in church either. Consequently, the filter these ladies have as it relates to men is pretty bad.

I ask you this: What escape does a woman gifted with any form of beauty have? The scriptures tell us that our Father always, in every temptation provides a way of escape. What escape do these women have when it comes to positive intimacy with men? How are they ever to know what a genuine protective embrace from a male figure is supposed to be if all men, especially the 'godly' men, are worried about the lust of the flesh or what their church members or spouses may think?

This is not a license for marital partners, or those who are single, to seek out the most attractive or physically appealing person in the room and find ways to demonstrate 'the Love of Christ". No, this is not about attraction, sex, lust or relationship envy. All those words are **death.**

The real purpose we are honing in on relationships with the opposite sex is to offer a reality check. If you were asked, "*Are you operating as the Light of Christ?*" Most will look at their lives and respond with something along the lines of, '*Yes sir, I certainly am. I pray almost every day. I fast and worship; and I refrain from sin. Light is all in me!*' Really? Who else is effected by the shining beacon of light within you?

A beacon works best for those lost in darkness. To shine out to those lost, and tossed to and fro on the waves of circumstance. The Light brightly declares, "This is the way to safety!" Likewise, this message is strictly to point out what is in you – the Light, and who needs it – the world. We are identifying that those in world are actually in the highways and byways.   Those are the prostitutes, drug addicts, adulterous co-workers or absolute strangers you meet every day. It matters not that their occupation or lifestyle is shady, or that they may be the opposite gender and attracted (attractive) to you.   These things are all secular values and pale in comparison to a conscious mind that knows that they are the Light of Christ, and were made to be a way of escape.

It is only our operating in unconditional Love that demonstrates to others that we are disciples (John 13:35). Our jobs are to be carriers of the Light. This is our instruction; LET our Light shine.   We do not have to forcefully or proactively try and seek certain places to shine. Wherever we are, that is where the Light is.   And guess what?   If Light is present, then darkness **must** flee to the cracks and low places. The more attention we give to the Light, the brighter everything is, including our partnerships.   They will only know that you are a disciple by the way we Love one another. Allow the Father to use your marriage.   Be very open and transparent with each other about the triumphs and shortcomings and watch the Father take your marriage partnership to another level. We need each other and God will always meet the needs of your relationship.   If you desire to save your life, then lose it in Him.   Again, they will only know you are a disciple by the way you Love one another.   It is not about you.   It is about what is in you.   **Beloved, you are released to let them see, and let them know.**

13

...by This They Will Know

"*Go ye into all the world and teach all nations!*" ...the battle cry of all evangelists and missionaries across the globe. Most of us have heard that we are to preach and believe in the Great Commission. We know we are called to make disciples of all nations and to teach all nations and people groups, and as the Bible states in **Matthew 28:19**, we should, **"Make disciples of all nations..."** However, the burning question then becomes, what exactly is the characteristic of a disciple? If the command is to make disciples, then we need to know what a disciple of Christ looks like. Make disciples of ALL nations, and teach ALL nations is a pretty broad and ambiguous mandate at first glance. Having five children and leading teams in sports and on the mission field, I know vision must be clearly understood if those following are expected to act as one. As we search the scriptures and see Christ refer to disciples, we must understand what 'making disciples' means and how we practically follow this command given to every believer.

As a disciple of Christ you are here for others, and not only for the saved or those that have understanding of the faith but as a Light set to shine forth on whomever may need it. You are not here only to serve those of your own household. No, you are not. You are called to a life that seeks and saves those that are lost. Christ said in *Luke 19:10 "...for the Son of Man has come to seek and to save that which was lost."* This mandate is what fueled the character of Christ and caused him to fully operate in His assignment wherever He went. Wherever Jesus was, He was on assignment. Not just at home or amongst the brethren, but wherever He went He was a representation of Heaven. This is exactly how we are called to live, outside ourselves and esteeming others higher.

The only direct description of the character trait of a disciple of Christ is found in John 13. *"By this they will know you are my disciples, if you have love for one another."- John 13:35* This concept is certainly not strange. It is frequently heard but somehow completely lost in application. If we are to fulfill the assignment and call of Christ on our lives, we must hold onto this understanding. Ask the heavenly Father for a personal revelation of what His Love looks like in your life and inside your circumstances.

If He were to have your body, your gender, your height, your network of friends, your job status, community position and ministry, what would His daily actions look like? How would He allow people to know He was the Light? The world will only know you are His disciple by the way you Love on others. If you are to embody the character of Christ, you will have to find a way to break limitations, understand that human wisdom is confused by the simplicity of Christ, and defy secular logic.

Sound superhuman?

Well maybe, but again, this is the narrow path and difficult way. You must make a conscious decision to walk on this road. You do not just find yourself affecting the lives of everyone around you for the good by default. It happens by being in a conscious state of understanding who you are - *Light of the world* and what is in you - *Mind of Christ*. The world may live their lives to make things better for themselves and more convenient for their own families, but self-preservation is not your assignment.

Self-preservation really only serves the interest of self and you are not created just to benefit you or your family. You were made to Love. He desires you to shine brightly with His glory to be seen by all nations, not just within your family. Be empowered to live proactively by your faith and less reactive to the stimulus responses of the flesh. By this they will know your Light and will be able to glorify your Father in heaven. This proactive nature, will keep you from being cheated out of the benefits of having the mind of Christ. *Colossians 2: 8* says, *"<u>Beware</u> lest anyone cheat you through philosophy and empty deceit, according to the traditions of men, according to the basic principles of the world, and not according to Christ."* The adversary knows that once you have the mind of Jesus nothing will be kept from you. You will not be able to be cheated through philosophy or traditions of men. Contrariwise, you will start to demonstrate the very things Jesus did on Earth. You will have His mind and His proactive nature. You will be so far from the lower level thinking of the world that people will ask, "What belief are you?" "Why are you so different?" "How do these things not affect you?" The world around you will not know how to respond to the authority of Love being demonstrated.

Imagine not being reactive to the desires of the flesh. Envision yourself understanding that you are the Light of the world (a medic), and wherever you go you are there to shine Hope, Love, Peace and Joy. You are not turned off by darkness or physical appearance, nor are you turned on by what you see. You are not reactive to the opposite sex and your mind is able to hear assignments from heaven in the midst of distraction. Beloved, this is how the world will know who is in you. You do not have to force your witness. Light is already in you, let it shine and let the world be drawn to the Light of Christ in you.

As you focus more on Him than you do on the evil and darkness in the world, His Light will increase. The more attention you pay to Him, the bigger He becomes in you. *8 Draw nigh to God, and he will draw nigh to you... - James 4:8* Do not be overly focused on avoiding the darkness of current times. If you focus too much on it you will be in danger of losing your ministry and you will not be able to help those whom need the Light of Christ most. Be emboldened to reject the traditions of men that do not line up with scripture. It is not worth it. You must flee from any situation that causes you to lose the mind of Christ. That is the spirit of anti-Christ and it no longer defines who you are. You are no longer subject to the wisdom and traditions of man. You are conscious of who you are and what is in you. You are not called to be palatable to the flesh but you are called to embody the character of Christ in every relationship, interaction and circumstance.

Beloved, old things are passed away. The low level thought process that used to cause you to think like the average secular good natured person is not for you anymore. You are being called up. You are now operating in a higher thought life through the mind of Christ. The things that hindered Christ in you and limited you from growing in impact are now gone. The world no longer defines who you are or how you operate. The basic principles of the secular world can never establish the boundaries or operations of a child of God. You are breaking free from the bonds of anything that you have held onto simply because it was familiar. Now, you are content with Christ. Everything you do is lined up with His nature, His character and His experiences. All visual stimuli that has programmed your thinking from youth to adult is being reprogrammed and your past-files are now the experiences of Christ. Old things are passed away and all things have become new. Selfish desire no longer has you bound to your flesh. The differences between male and female is no longer a distraction. You understand that one needs the other to grow and develop properly. We need each other as family, as mothers, brothers, sisters and fathers; in all purity (1 Timothy 5:2). You are now functioning outside physical attraction and acknowledge the truth of why you were created and what responsibility you have in the life of another.

Beloved, the Love of God will show you how to govern your heart. There is a lot to be said about a person that governs their spirit well. The Bible tells us in *Proverbs 25:28, "He that does not have rule over his own spirit is like a city broken down, and without walls."* By walking in the Light of Christ you are now conscious everywhere you go. Your body is under your authority and you are no longer like an establishment that has no boundaries with everything that is valuable and worthy open and EXPOSED to your enemy.

Sister, you are a kept woman that is available to be used of the Father to assist those around you. You are no longer open to participate in every situation that offers you promotion through sensual manipulation. You are a Virtuous Woman empowered to minister Christ wherever you go.

Brother, you are a mighty man of Valor that is anchored in spirit and seeks the greater good of those around you. You are no longer open to the whims of any attraction that comes near you. You are the master of your spirit and conscious in every situation, no matter what the flesh may desire.

Beloved, let us Love one another. Let us truly Love in deed and be conscious, confident and determined to rule our own spirit well. Let us capture every thought whether it come when you are at a restaurant, at the beach, at the gym, watching a movie, viewing commercials, watching a T.V. show, browsing online video streams or watching YouTube. Let us no longer be a slave to a society of reaction. Let us unplug from the Matrix of mass media and flesh pleasing entertainment. Today you are being called up and called out. You have been unplugged from the systems of this world. *What used to be the school of thought that validated your every judgment and value system is no longer good for you. Now you are a new creature.*

Go forth. Restore confidence in your Spirit. Restore confidence in the Truth. This will enable you to continue to stand firm, no matter the circumstances. You will be able to look at secular mass media without compromise and declare that you will no longer use their programming to define what is good or evil. No man can judge the Father, so let no man judge the Father who lives **within** you. Go forth in boldness and declare that the Truth you have within - is enough.

Go forth. Declare that no matter how unrighteous it makes you look to the judgments of secular desire and temporary pleasure - He is enough. You need not the validation of men. You are a royal priesthood, a peculiar people. Continue to walk in your purpose and let your Light shine brightly.

Go forth, and as a child embrace the simplicity of higher thinking and watch as it confounds the wisdom of this system and breaks the chains of darkness off every area of your life. Beloved, I Love You, and pray that you receive this impartation of boldness to Love as Christ Loved.

Go forth. Truly Love without inhibition of darkness ..."*by this they will know you are my disciples*" – *John 13:35*

Your Brother, eg

Message to the Reader

First off, congratulations for finding this manuscript. Thank you for considering this reading worthy of attention and taking the time to hear the heart of the Father for ministry. If you completed the book, I pray an impartation of understanding concerning the Power of Agape Love has been received; it is now yours to walk in. Most of the reviews and feedback received thus far have been overwhelmingly positive. After reading this book, people are understanding the plans of the adversary a little clearer and allowing their Light to shine. To that I say, Praise Him and Hallelujah. That is the intent and design of this reading. It was created to illuminate the plan of the enemy through sexualization and provoke a response of indignation. I have personally felt bewitched in how the body of Christ has approached gender relations and sexuality. Sexuality is something the Father wants to redeem and show that nothing is hidden from Him; not even our relational intimacy. With the mind of Christ shaping our approach to sexuality, not only can marriages heal and be restored, but single young adults and maturing adolescents can discover the hidden ills of accepting the Matrix of cultural social acceptance as reality. While our aim is to look more like Christ, there are still others whom may be more concerned with the fig leaf fallen nature of man and cannot escape the cultural state of over-sexualization. They believe we should guard ourselves and not venture into areas mentioned in the book. I get it. I understand. However, Fear not. The aim is Christ and nothing about the mind of Christ allows for selfish desire or passions of the flesh to have the seat of preeminence. We are vessels, containers of Light and beacons of grace shining in the darkness. The aim is to Shine. The closer you get to Christ, the less you see of Jew or Greek, bond or free, and male or female. The closer we get to walking in the mind of Christ, the more we recognize that the world truly is bound in darkness and needs exactly what is inside us. We must grow and understand His ways and His thoughts are not synonymous to the mindset of social acceptance. As we grasp His mind, persecution will come, but again, do not be afraid. Only deepen your walk with Him. Spend more time with Holy Spirit and see greater dimensions of His grace on your life. Beloved, time is short. Fear not those that can kill the body, but rather concern yourself with your eternal position. Let us- Love one another.

eg

...eternal perspective

Feel free to learn more on the web www.charlesgoss.org or write via email bythistheywillknow@gmail.com